WANG SHAOQIANG

SCENO GRAPHICS

Set Design & Papercraft Art: A New Graphic Design Approach

Grafisme 3D fait main. Diseño gráfico 3D hecho a mano. Cenografia gráfica: novo design 3D

promopress

SCENOGRAPHICS

Set Design & Papercraft Art: A New Graphic Design Approach
Grafisme 3D fait main
Diseño gráfico 3D hecho a mano
Cenografia gráfica: novo design 3D

English preface revised by: Tom Corkett
Translators of the preface: Marie-Pierre Teuler French translation /
Jesús de Cos Pinto Spanish translation /
Élcio Carillo Portuguese (Brazilian) translation
Cover design: Retina & Retinette

PROMOPRESS is a brand of:
Promotora de Prensa Internacional S.A.
C/ Ausiàs March, 124
08013 Barcelona, Spain
Phone: +34 93 245 14 64
Fax: +34 93 265 48 83
info@promopress.es
www.promopress.es
www.promopresseditions.com
Facebook: Promopress Editions
Twitter: Promopress Editions @PromopressEd

Sponsored by Design 360°
– Concept and Design Magazine

Edited and produced by
Sandu Publishing Co., Ltd.
Book design, concepts & art direction by
Sandu Publishing Co., Ltd.
info@sandupublishing.com

Cover project by SNASK

ISBN 978-84-15967-31-6

Printed in China

CONTENTS

PREFACE

Set Design: As I See It

Linnea Apelqvist
Set Designer and Prop Stylist

Paul Valéry's belief that "the greatest freedom comes from the greatest strictness" is very true in set design, where the creative process starts with a brief. The brief, or a set of rules if you like, gives the project a direction and can be anything from a text, an idea or a selection of images to something as abstract as a colour or a texture. Your job is to communicate this brief in a visual way, turning it into a physical, three-dimensional space – that is, your set. The manner in which this manifests itself can vary greatly from project to project, ranging from the very abstract to the realistically figurative. This process is often a collaboration with other people, for instance a director or a photographer. The set is there to visually engage your audience and to emotionally draw the viewer into your world, creating a platform for the protagonist.

As a set designer and prop stylist I mainly do still-life photography. A still life is a collection of objects assembled and styled in a very considered and precise way. When doing commercial work you are most likely selling a product – this could be a selection of fashion accessories, a group of chairs or a collection of wallpapers – and you have to make it look its best and show it off in a way that is interesting and relevant to your set. Personal projects differ in that you have complete freedom to do what you like. There is no client to please or products to show off, and therefore the project often takes on a more artistic manner.

When working with photography as a medium every millimetre matters, as where you place your props makes a difference to the composition and the overall feeling of the image. Textures, colours and shapes all play a part in creating an image. Light also plays a vital role, and a good photographer will use it in a way that beautifully sculpts his or her set and brings the image to life. Optical illusions can likewise have a big part to play and can in my view make things really interesting. There is often a lot going on behind the scenes – making the props balance or appear to be hanging freely in the air, for example – that you can't see in the final image. It takes a lot of patience, time and effort to create a still-life image, something that many people don't realize.

In this field each project you take on is unique and comes with its own set of problems for you to solve. One day you might be outside gluing flowers to branches, while the next you could be delicately arranging peppercorns in a neat line, or standing in a large, dark studio, covered in paint. This is a big part of what makes the job interesting and pushes you to develop as a set designer.

Set design is not all fun and glamour, though. There is a very demanding side to it too. A lot of your time is devoted to running around shops and prop houses, packing and unpacking props and products before and after each shoot and carrying heavy stuff from one place to another and back again. Luckily, a lot of it is a collective effort, and you will have a great team of assistants to help you.

I feel that set design is growing as an art form and that the boundaries for what it can be are evolving. In many instances the notion of what a set designer is expands to include the role of art director, which brings greater freedom to come up with ideas and concepts for the project. Set designers come from a variety of backgrounds, and the job is very multidisciplinary. It's no longer just something done for a play or a film; there are now endless possibilities for designing environments for events, commercial spaces, window displays, exhibitions, trade shows, receptions, lobbies and many other places. Set designers are starting to get more credibility for their creative input and hard work – something I truly believe that we deserve!

PRÉFACE

La décoration-scénographie telle que je l'entends

Linnea Apelqvist
Décoratrice-scénographe et styliste photo

Paul Valéry a dit que « la plus grande liberté naît de la plus grande rigueur ». Cette maxime s'applique aussi à la décoration-scénographie où le processus créatif commence toujours par un concept. C'est une sorte de cadre définissant l'orientation du projet. Cela peut être un texte, une idée, une série d'images ou bien quelque chose de complètement abstrait comme une couleur ou une texture. Notre mission est de traduire visuellement ce concept dans un espace à trois dimensions: le décor. Le résultat varie d'un projet à l'autre et peut aller de l'abstraction totale au réalisme figuratif. L'élaboration du décor s'effectue généralement en collaboration avec d'autres personnes, par exemple, un directeur ou un photographe. Le décor doit attirer visuellement le public et l'entraîner émotionnellement dans un autre monde qui mettra en scène le sujet choisi.

En tant que décoratrice-scénographe et styliste photo, je fais surtout des photos de nature morte. Une nature morte est une collection d'objets réunis et arrangés d'une manière précise suivant un objectif donné. Un photographe publicitaire s'intéresse principalement à des produits à vendre, par exemple, des accessoires de mode, un jeu de chaises ou une collection de papiers peints. Il choisit une présentation qui les mette en valeur dans le décor fixé. Le cas d'un projet photo personnel est complètement différent. On est entièrement libre parce qu'on n'a pas à plaire au client ni à servir un produit. Le résultat est souvent plus artistique.

Lorsque notre outil est un appareil photo, chaque millimètre compte. L'endroit que l'on choisit pour placer les accessoires influence la composition et l'atmosphère qui se dégage de la scène. Les textures, les couleurs et les formes participent à la création de l'image. La lumière joue également un rôle fondamental. Un bon photographe saura en tirer partie pour sculpter magnifiquement son décor et donner vie au tableau. De même, les illusions optiques ont aussi une grande importance et je pense qu'elles ajoutent de l'intérêt à l'image. Derrière une photo il y a généralement un énorme travail en coulisse, par exemple, pour équilibrer la composition ou pour qu'un objet ait l'air de flotter dans l'espace. La plupart des gens ne se rendent pas compte que l'élaboration d'une nature morte exige beaucoup de patience, de temps et d'efforts.

Dans notre domaine, chaque projet est différent et pose de nouveaux problèmes qu'il va falloir résoudre. Vous pouvez un jour travailler en extérieur à coller des fleurs sur une branche et le lendemain aligner soigneusement des épis de maïs en file indienne ou encore vous retrouver entièrement couvert de peinture au milieu d'un immense studio plongé la pénombre. La variété de la décoration-scénographie et du stylisme photo est ce qui fait l'intérêt de ce travail et nous pousse à choisir cette activité.

Cependant ce métier n'a pas que des bons côtés. Il est aussi très exigeant. On passe beaucoup de temps à écumer les boutiques et les magasins d'accessoires, à déballer et remballer les éléments du décor avant et après chaque prise de vue et à transporter des charges lourdes d'un endroit à l'autre. Heureusement, une grande partie de ce travail se fait en équipe et vous avez des assistants pour vous aider.

J'ai le sentiment que la décoration-scénographie est en train de devenir un art à part entière et que ses limites reculent. Le décorateur-scénographe joue bien souvent le rôle de directeur artistique lui donnant une plus grande liberté créative par rapport au projet. La plupart des professionnels ont des formations très diverses et le travail exige du talent dans différentes disciplines. Le décorateur-scénographe ne se limite plus au théâtre et au cinéma. Les possibilités qui s'offrent à lui sont infinies. Il peut créer des décors pour des événements, des espaces commerciaux, des vitrines, des expositions, des foires commerciales, des réceptions, des halls d'hôtels et bien d'autres lieux encore. Le décorateur-scénographe est de plus en plus reconnu pour sa créativité et sa capacité de travail, et c'est entièrement mérité!

PREFACIO

Diseño de escenarios: mi visión

Linnea Apelqvist
Diseñadora de escenarios y estilista de utillería

Paul Valéry's belief that "the greatest freedom comes from the greatest strictness" is very true in set design, where the creative process starts with a brief. The brief, or a set of rules if you like, gives the project a direction and can be anything from a text, an idea or a selection of images to something as abstract as a colour or a texture. Your job is to communicate this brief in a visual way, turning it into a physical, three-dimensional space – that is, your set. The manner in which this manifests itself can vary greatly from project to project, ranging from the very abstract to the realistically figurative. This process is often a collaboration with other people, for instance a director or a photographer. The set is there to visually engage your audience and to emotionally draw the viewer into your world, creating a platform for the protagonist.

As a set designer and prop stylist I mainly do still-life photography. A still life is a collection of objects assembled and styled in a very considered and precise way. When doing commercial work you are most likely selling a product – this could be a selection of fashion accessories, a group of chairs or a collection of wallpapers – and you have to make it look its best and show it off in a way that is interesting and relevant to your set. Personal projects differ in that you have complete freedom to do what you like. There is no client to please or products to show off, and therefore the project often takes on a more artistic manner.

When working with photography as a medium every millimetre matters, as where you place your props makes a difference to the composition and the overall feeling of the image. Textures, colours and shapes all play a part in creating an image. Light also plays a vital role, and a good photographer will use it in a way that beautifully sculpts his or her set and brings the image to life. Optical illusions can likewise have a big part to play and can in my view make things really interesting. There is often a lot going on behind the scenes – making the props balance or appear to be hanging freely in the air, for example – that you can't see in the final image. It takes a lot of patience, time and effort to create a still-life image, something that many people don't realize.

In this field each project you take on is unique and comes with its own set of problems for you to solve. One day you might be outside gluing flowers to branches, while the next you could be delicately arranging peppercorns in a neat line, or standing in a large, dark studio, covered in paint. This is a big part of what makes the job interesting and pushes you to develop as a set designer.

Set design is not all fun and glamour, though. There is a very demanding side to it too. A lot of your time is devoted to running around shops and prop houses, packing and unpacking props and products before and after each shoot and carrying heavy stuff from one place to another and back again. Luckily, a lot of it is a collective effort, and you will have a great team of assistants to help you.

I feel that set design is growing as an art form and that the boundaries for what it can be are evolving. In many instances the notion of what a set designer is expands to include the role of art director, which brings greater freedom to come up with ideas and concepts for the project. Set designers come from a variety of backgrounds, and the job is very multidisciplinary. It's no longer just something done for a play or a film; there are now endless possibilities for designing environments for events, commercial spaces, window displays, exhibitions, trade shows, receptions, lobbies and many other places. Set designers are starting to get more credibility for their creative input and hard work – something I truly believe that we deserve!

PREFÁCIO

Design de cenários: a minha visão

Linnea Apelqvist
Designer de cenários e estilista de acessórios

Paul Valéry a dit que « la plus grande liberté naît de la plus grande rigueur ». Cette maxime s'applique aussi à la décoration-scénographie où le processus créatif commence toujours par un concept. C'est une sorte de cadre définissant l'orientation du projet. Cela peut être un texte, une idée, une série d'images ou bien quelque chose de complètement abstrait comme une couleur ou une texture. Notre mission est de traduire visuellement ce concept dans un espace à trois dimensions: le décor. Le résultat varie d'un projet à l'autre et peut aller de l'abstraction totale au réalisme figuratif. L'élaboration du décor s'effectue généralement en collaboration avec d'autres personnes, par exemple, un directeur ou un photographe. Le décor doit attirer visuellement le public et l'entraîner émotionnellement dans un autre monde qui mettra en scène le sujet choisi.

En tant que décoratrice-scénographe et styliste photo, je fais surtout des photos de nature morte. Une nature morte est une collection d'objets réunis et arrangés d'une manière précise suivant un objectif donné. Un photographe publicitaire s'intéresse principalement à des produits à vendre, par exemple, des accessoires de mode, un jeu de chaises ou une collection de papiers peints. Il choisit une présentation qui les mette en valeur dans le décor fixé. Le cas d'un projet photo personnel est complètement différent. On est entièrement libre parce qu'on n'a pas à plaire au client ni à servir un produit. Le résultat est souvent plus artistique.

Lorsque notre outil est un appareil photo, chaque millimètre compte. L'endroit que l'on choisit pour placer les accessoires influence la composition et l'atmosphère qui se dégage de la scène. Les textures, les couleurs et les formes participent à la création de l'image. La lumière joue également un rôle fondamental. Un bon photographe saura en tirer partie pour sculpter magnifiquement son décor et donner vie au tableau. De même, les illusions optiques ont aussi une grande importance et je pense qu'elles ajoutent de l'intérêt à l'image. Derrière une photo il y a généralement un énorme travail en coulisse, par exemple, pour équilibrer la composition ou pour qu'un objet ait l'air de flotter dans l'espace. La plupart des gens ne se rendent pas compte que l'élaboration d'une nature morte exige beaucoup de patience, de temps et d'efforts.

Dans notre domaine, chaque projet est différent et pose de nouveaux problèmes qu'il va falloir résoudre. Vous pouvez un jour travailler en extérieur à coller des fleurs sur une branche et le lendemain aligner soigneusement des épis de maïs en file indienne ou encore vous retrouver entièrement couvert de peinture au milieu d'un immense studio plongé la pénombre. La variété de la décoration-scénographie et du stylisme photo est ce qui fait l'intérêt de ce travail et nous pousse à choisir cette activité.

Cependant ce métier n'a pas que des bons côtés. Il est aussi très exigeant. On passe beaucoup de temps à écumer les boutiques et les magasins d'accessoires, à déballer et remballer les éléments du décor avant et après chaque prise de vue et à transporter des charges lourdes d'un endroit à l'autre. Heureusement, une grande partie de ce travail se fait en équipe et vous avez des assistants pour vous aider.

J'ai le sentiment que la décoration-scénographie est en train de devenir un art à part entière et que ses limites reculent. Le décorateur-scénographe joue bien souvent le rôle de directeur artistique lui donnant une plus grande liberté créative par rapport au projet. La plupart des professionnels ont des formations très diverses et le travail exige du talent dans différentes disciplines. Le décorateur-scénographe ne se limite plus au théâtre et au cinéma. Les possibilités qui s'offrent à lui sont infinies. Il peut créer des décors pour des événements, des espaces commerciaux, des vitrines, des expositions, des foires commerciales, des réceptions, des halls d'hôtels et bien d'autres lieux encore. Le décorateur-scénographe est de plus en plus reconnu pour sa créativité et sa capacité de travail, et c'est entièrement mérité!

9

01

Malmö Festival 2014

Design Agency // SNASK
Creative Direction // Fredrik Öst
Art Direction // Jens Nilsson
Copywriter // Alexandra Arvidsson
Photography // Anders Sipinen, Nils Bergendahl

Behind The Scenes

"IT TURNED INTO AN ART INSTALLATION OF THE FESTIVAL FOR THE VISITORS TO INTERACT WITH, SIT ON AND EVEN JUMP ON."

Assignment

The Malmö Festival is Scandinavia's largest city festival during eight days with more than 1,5 million visitors. 2014 was the 30th anniversary and SNASK fifth year as their agency. It's financed by tax payers so it has no entry fee or tickets. It's basically culture made for everyone to experience. They decided to make something spectacular that would blow people's minds and be worthy of the 30th anniversary.

Idea

Recent years SNASK had made very tactile posters entirely made by hand with a sense for the viewer that he/she could actually "be" in the poster. For the 30th anniversary, they made a poster that would be an entire area for the people to climb on and interact with. They really wanted to make it huge and get people to actually sit on it. So they made it extremely sturdy and weather proof as well as different heights so it would be easy to climb.

Process

It started with sketching and designing in Illustrator. After that they made a model in a 3D software just to see how high up they needed to be in the air in order to photograph it properly. If too close it would get bad angles on the edges. After that they sent files to wood machines that cut out the design in really huge proportions. A carpenter then put everything together in a flawless manner and painted it in the colours they ordered. Then they went down to Malmö to build up and shoot the whole installation in a skylift 30 meters up in the air. They also had to plan the actual photoshoot with the shadow from the sun. They started at 6 am and knew that they had to start photographing at 12 am and two hours forward before the shadow would fall in the direction (according to their design sense).

Result

The art installation (13x8 meters) took roughly 900 hours, used 14 people, 10 000 nails, 175 litres of paint and 280 plywood sheets. The result was very exciting since it's always a pleasure to work with graphic design that is taken out into reality. After the photoshoot in May the installation was put in a warehouse until the festival in mid August where it was placed as a physical area of interaction and climbing.

02

Swedish Handicraft

Design Agency // SNASK
Creative Direction // Fredrik Öst
Art Direction // Jens Nilsson

"THE GRAPHIC IDENTITY AND COMMUNICATION IS NOW HANDMADE, REPRESENTING EVERYTHING THAT THEIR MEMBERS LIVE AND BREATHE."

Assignment

Established in 1912 the National Association of Swedish Handicraft Societies (SHR) celebrates its 100th anniversary in 2012. The organisation consists of 8 retail shops, 22 regional offices and over 17 000 members. When all lights are on, they are going to change people's perception of what handicraft means in today's society. What once only meant a sustainable way of living, creating your own arts and home appliances, have now expanded to include D.I.Y, Guerilla, Craftivism, Recycling and everything made by hand really.

Idea

Armed with SHR's existing brand platform, SNASK realized their brand essence: "with our hands we shape the future. We turned what to communicate into how to communicate, creating a visual identity and communication based around 'Everything SHR says, we say by hand'."

Process

By engaging and inspiring the whole movement SNASK managed to unite everyone under one new brand, Hemslöjden. To make the visual identity genuine, they engaged SHR's own members in creating the logo.

Result

SNASK united one Sweden's oldest and most genuine grassroot movements, under one brand idea fittingly to the 100th anniversary. Every regional office now uses one coherent visual identity with pride, fellowing brand guidelines to produce branded material with accuracy.

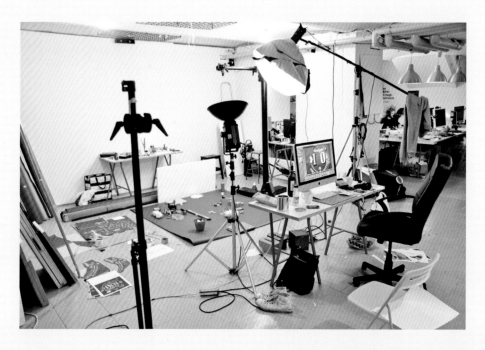

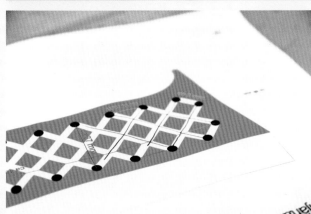

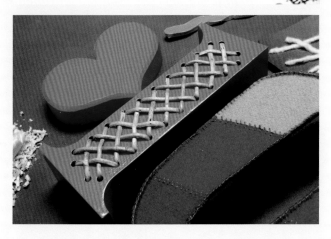

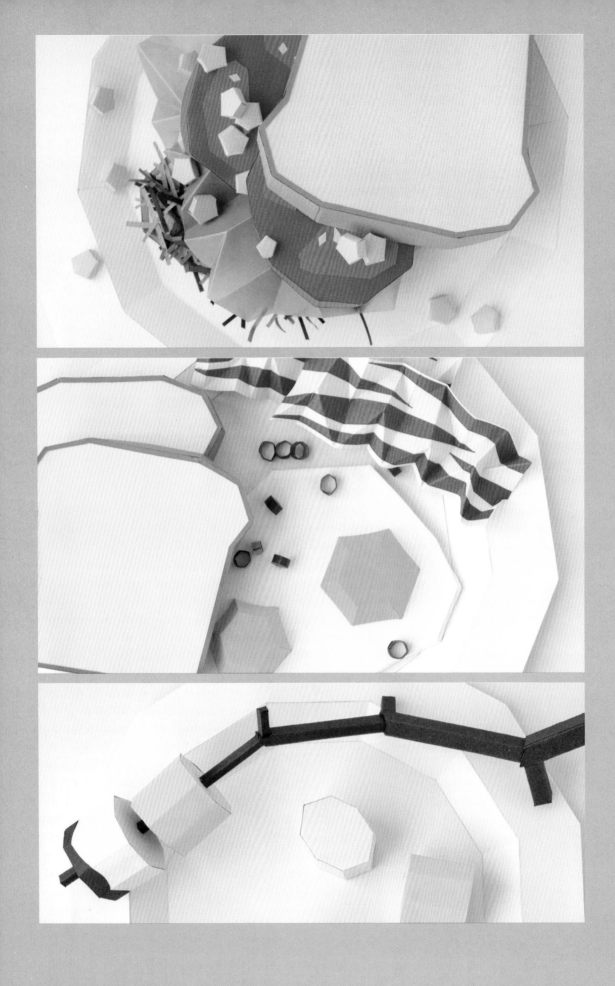

Taste The Font

Design Agency // PRIM PRIM
Creative Team // Migle Vasiliauskaite, Kotryna Zilinskiene,
Linas Mikoliunas, Vytenis Zilinskas

Behind The Scenes

"EACH RECIPE WAS CHOSEN TO REFERENCE THE HISTORY OF THE FONT."

Assignment

A few years ago two PRIM PRIM studio creatives raised a question – is it possible to describe the taste of the font? That is how the "special dinner project" Taste the Font began.

Idea

The idea of Taste the Font came unexpectedly – once they just thought that fried breakfast eggs have the very same character as Times Roman font. The idea was so crazy that they started this project immediately.
The goal was to educate people in fonts while arousing one of five human senses – taste. Because of the emerging connections through the taste, the information remains longer in human brain. It is a very unusual way to help people to be more aware of the fonts.

Process

The people working on the project were neither professional cooks nor food photographers – just a couple of crazy designers. The fun for them was in characterizing the font by choosing the most suitable dish for it, then writing the story of the choice and the cooking processes for the tastethefont. com blog.
Moreover, each recipe was chosen to reference the history of the font, making the project not only delicious, but healthy for the brain as well.
The project continued from 2011 to 2012 and each font imagined as a dish was presented in tasthethefont.com blog; however, in 2013 Vilnius Design Week organisers asked PRIM PRIM to make an exhibition of Taste the Font for public display. Two architects joined the team and transformed Times, Courier New and Comic Sans recipes into detailed paper-craft dishes. Paper models weren't the initial concept, but the designers simply couldn't think of any other way to show font dishes, so that they would keep their freshness for longer than a day. The biggest challenge was the creation of a huge paper tongue meant to be a highlight of the exposition.

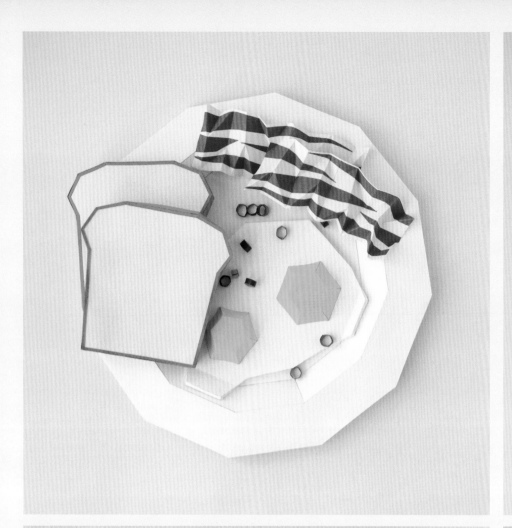

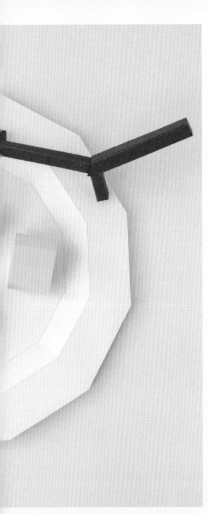

Result

The project received heavy attention from the public and press. The team was also asked to leave the artwork on display after the Design Week event was over. Taste the Font was featured in designboom.com portal and after it spread in a lot of various design, food design portals and blogs. It was featured in magazines such as *IdN*, *Fricotè*, *Business Punk* and published in several design books.

Malmö Festival 2013

Design Agency // SNASK
Creative Direction // Fredrik Öst
Art Direction // Jens Nilsson
Design // Richard Gray (Paper
        Bunny made by Chloé
        Fleury)

The 29th edition of Malmöfestivalen, Scandinavias largest city festival, had "paper" as a theme. The whole city of Malmö, as well as every piece of communication and branding, needed to get a coat of paper to communicate the chosen theme.

SNASK created a visual concept where everything was made by hand in paper. For a month cutting, folding, gluing and modelling became the everyday task. One challenge was to create objects in paper that would be reproduced in gigantic scale in cardboard and taken to the streets of Malmö. The designers added the feeling of the material by partially ripping up and apart some of the pieces they produced. They made films in stop motion for advertisement as well as for the screens of the big stage in-between concerts. Countless paper models and paper portraits also covered the magazine, which went out to everyone in Malmö (about 500k people).

The festival became a huge success and some visitors called it the best of the 29 years of existence. The paper theme was visible everywhere, from screens and newspapers, to the very streets in the shape of the giant cardboard models.

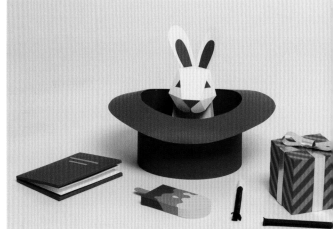

Carneval Poster

Creative Direction // Áron Filkey, Daniel Balint,
Kristof Kiss-Benedek
Photography // Donát Kékesi

Poster series for the carnival event of Moholy-Nagy University of Art and Design (MOME).
The designers combined design photography with creative paper manipulation to produce
these impressive pieces of paper art.

MOME × KÉPZŐ
FARSANG
2012 MÁRCIUS 1.
MERLIN

MOME × KÉPZŐ
FARSANG
2012 MÁRCIUS 1.
MERLIN

MOME × KÉPZŐ
FARSANG
2012 MÁRCIUS 1.
MERLIN

MOME × KÉPZŐ
FARSANG
2012 MÁRCIUS 1.
MERLIN

The Border

<u>Design</u> // Carolin Wanitzek
<u>Photography</u> // Carolin Wanitzek

For a project called "die Grenze" in German which means "the border" in English, designer Carolin Wanitzek decided to visualize the edge between dream and reality, thinking about the little moment when you have a dream and wake up you are in both places and ask yourself what is real. The pictures precisely showed the edge between both worlds.

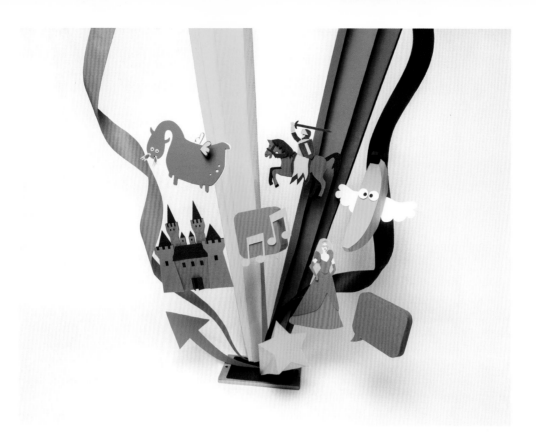

Scout Magazine

<u>Art Direction</u> // Cris Wiegandt
<u>Model Maker</u> // Cris Wiegandt, Nearly Normal
<u>Photography</u> // Cris Wiegandt, Nearly Normal

G+J Corporate Editors GmbH commissioned Cris Wiegandt to create diverse paper craft illustrations for the next edition of *Scout Magazine*. Working with a talented team of designers from the Nearly Normal Studio, she managed to mix tactile and handcrafted elements into three stunning compositions – all within a very tight deadline.

Tweet

<u>Art Direction</u> // Christian Ashton
<u>Graphic Design</u> // Christian Ashton
<u>Photography</u> // David Abrahams

A paper art project responding to the joy of reading. Designer Christian Ashton created an open page magazine spread from which the content jumped out in the form of paper art. Our captivated imagination takes us on a private journey through each book we read. He believes that it is the most organic way to really showcase the innocence and adventures we go through.

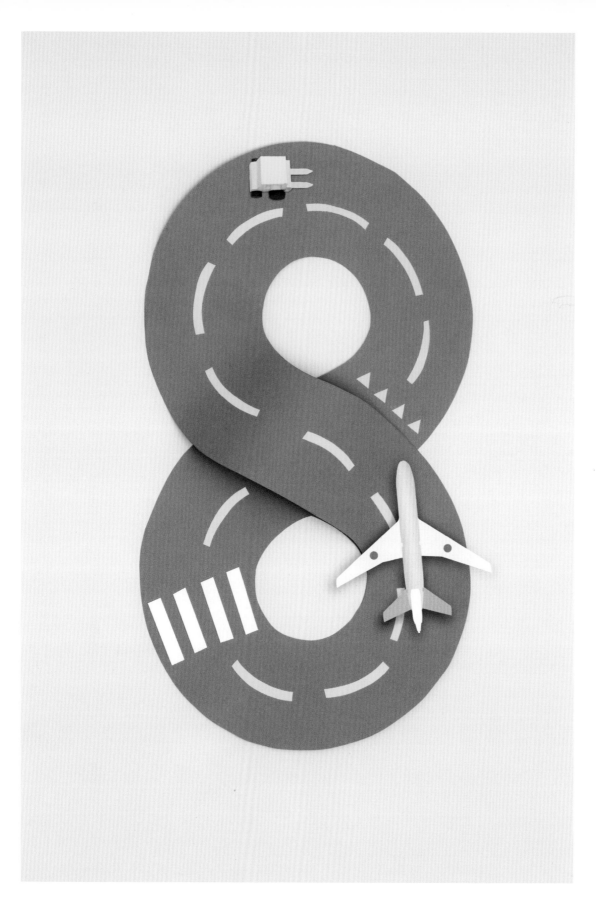

Skanska

Ad Agency // Lowe Brindfors
Photography // Carl Kleiner

Skanska AB, is a multinational construction and development company based in Sweden, where it is among the top three construction companies in the domestic market and the largest one when accounting for all markets, with approximately twice the revenue of the closest competitor. The company's head office is in Stockholm.

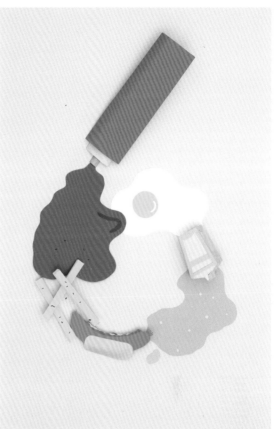

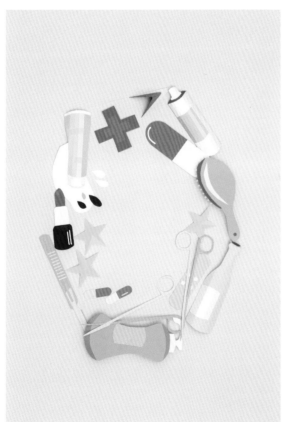

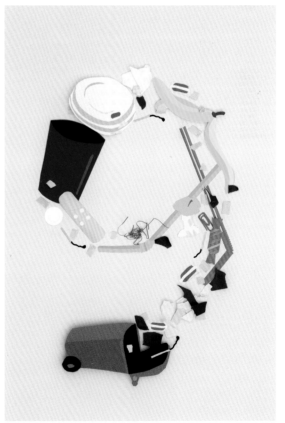

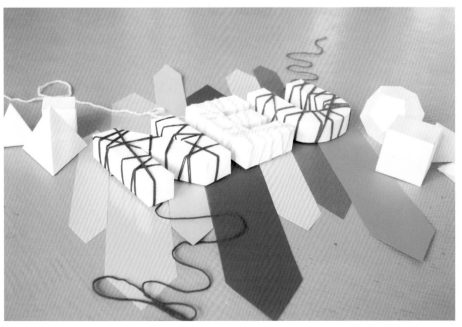

Subculture

Design // Carolin Wanitzek
Photography // Carolin Wanitzek

During a 100-days-trainee at Raum Mannheim, designer Carolin Wanitzek got the job to create a special cover design for the *Subculture* magazine. It is a small magazine which shows the readers all the dates for cultural events in the Rhein-Main-Neckar area in Germany. The designer chose the word NEU with the dynamical lines in the background, because they tried a restart.

YCN

<u>Photography</u> // Victoria Ling

YCN is an illustration agency, representing young artists. This was a commission to document a collection of work by their artists. The images were drawn together using the backgrounds with horizon line. Suitcase for Henrietta Swift; Shoes for Jessica Dance; Planes for Owen Gildersleeve.

Hello

<u>Design</u> // Amy Harris
<u>Photography</u> // Amy Harris

This was a self-promotion piece created by artist Amy Harris to engage with potential new clients in a fun, eye-catching and positive way. With bold, colourful typography at the centre of the design, characters were featured to add narrative and personality to the scene and capture a playful tone that represented the ethos of her work. The piece was turned into a printed poster, doubling as a small portfolio of work that was mailed to a select group of recipients.

Supermarket Sarah Wall

Design // Amy Harris
Photography // Amy Harris

Artist Amy Harris created a 'wall' of her artwork, products and props to showcase through this visually interactive online shop and creative platform for designers.

Monki Magazine

<u>Art Direction</u> // Cris Wiegandt
<u>Model Maker</u> // Cris Wiegandt

Cris Wiegandt was commissioned by Austria-based agency Plastic Media to create one Monki accessory in paper and a paper world for the final craft. The final work was printed in the September issue 2012 of *Monki Magazine*. Monki is a Swedish fashion label owned by H&M.

ArjoWiggins

<u>Ad Agency</u> // Reflex Agency
<u>Creative Direction</u> // Nicolas Champion
<u>Art Direction</u> // Frédéric Teysseire
<u>Set Design</u> // Hervé Sauvage
<u>Photography</u> // Grégoire Alexandre

ArjoWiggins is an international paper company that decided to celebrate the launch of its new paper range "Curious Collection." Photographer Grégoire Alexandre created a seriously fantastic photoshoot that was designed to portray the creativity behind the papers.

The New World
Business Class

Creative Direction // Sandy Poon
Art Direction // Adrian & Gidi
Design // Adrian & Gidi
Photography // Adrian & Gidi

Adrian & Gidi was commissioned by
KLM Asia WBC to photograph tactile
paper crafted sets showcasing certain
key elements that the business class
offers – bigger screens, more leg room,
privacy and comfort. All had to be
shot within the KLM colour palette. The
images were used for digital marketing
throughout Asia.

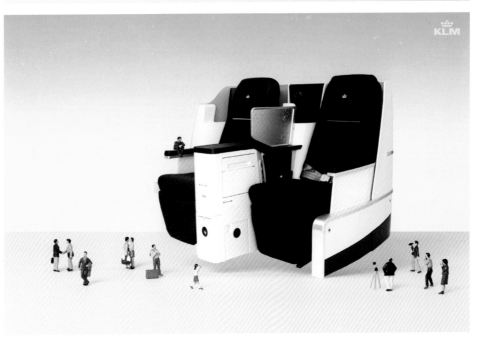

The Guardian Study

Design // Amy Harris
Photography // Amy Harris
Web Design & Build // Mohawk London

Artist Amy Harris created this study environment for *The Guardian's* new learning focused website: a platform for education and learning providers to offer information on opportunities for people with a desire to learn.

She hand crafted the scene from paper, and photographed it to create the final illustration, working with Mohawk London to bring it to life with interactive features, roll-over elements and a real-time clock.

Different objects represented areas such as 'fun courses' and 'postgraduate study,' each leading the user to subcategories and further information. Playful animations – e.g. a swinging pendulum and camera flash – were added to the scene, surprising and engaging the user in fun ways.

She later went on to make a life-sized version of this piece to promote the website, combining illustrative elements with real objects for an installation in *The Guardian's* space at the CASE conference 2014 in Edinburgh.

Geometry

<u>Art Direction</u> // Alexis Facca, Tom Joye
<u>Photography</u> // Tom Joye

This was a self-initiated project created by designer Alexis Facca who is specialised in paper art and set design. He feels that a geometric and colourful world full of evocative and exciting fun.

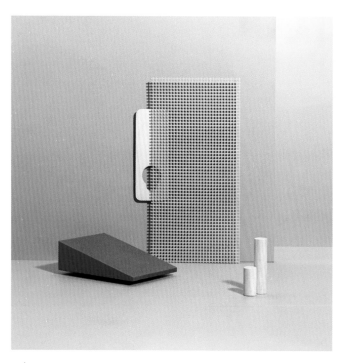

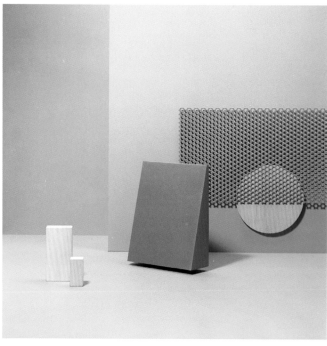

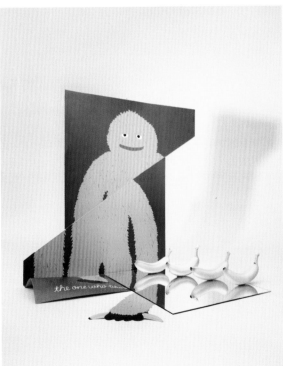

Human Empire

<u>Styling</u> // Elena Mora
<u>Photography</u> // Oliver Schwarzwald

Human Empire is a very nice concept store in Hamburg. They sell very nice poster and illustration made by different artists. These pictures were made to illustrate the cover of the new catalogue, as well as visual content for their website. The posters were folded in another way than what we are usually doing.

Pollination

Set Design // Hattie Newman
Art Direction // Gem Fletcher
Photography // Victoria Ling

This project was themed around the reproduction of plants to imagine romance and dating in the floral world.

ING Talks

Art Direction // Ryan Romanes
Design // Ryan Romanes
Paper Cutting // George Drury, Rayan Bekdash
Photography // Sydney Jones

Series of images created for Dubai creative community -ING. Each topic exploring the Talk's theme – Fail, Change, Search, Balance and Decide, images were applied to various formats, such as posters, advertising, postcards, etc. Compositions were created with paper, acrylic, polystyrene, cotton and toys found in local markets.

The Office

Art Direction // Alexis Facca, Tom Joye
Photography // Tom Joye

The office concept for advertising agency Walter R. Cooper. Founded in 1979, Walter R. Cooper became one of London's most celebrated agencies as it created glossy advertisements that often combined humour, music and sexual energy and came to define the Eighties. This story is a fiction.

Xmas Party Invite

Creative Direction // Oksana Valentelis
Model Maker // Oksana Valentelis
Photography // Oksana Valentelis

This was a Christmas party invite for advertising agency The Monkeys in Sydney. Because the party was on a boat, art director Oksana Valentelis made a paper scene showing a bunch of drunk monkeys out sailing and causing shenanigans. Those crazy monkeys.

World Cup

<u>Creative Direction</u> // Albertine van den Brink
<u>Design</u> // Adrian & Gidi
<u>Photography</u> // Adrian & Gidi

Adrian & Gidi was commissioned by the Dutch newspaper 'Het Parool' to shoot an image for their PS (inside magazine) cover and a second image to accompany the article about watching the world cup in cafe/bars in and around Amsterdam.

In-Vitro, Woolecule and Rhythm

<u>Design</u> // Adrian & Gidi
<u>Photography</u> // Adrian & Gidi

Next to advertising and editorial work, photography duo Adrian & Gidi loves to work on autonomous projects. They enjoy working with different materials like paper, wood, Styrofoam, etc. Free work gives them a chance to experiment with new techniques and ideas. Often they work towards an exhibition, publication or art-event to launch their free work. It also gives the project a deadline which is a good way to get things done. These works were shot for a selection of exhibitions in Amsterdam, the Netherlands.

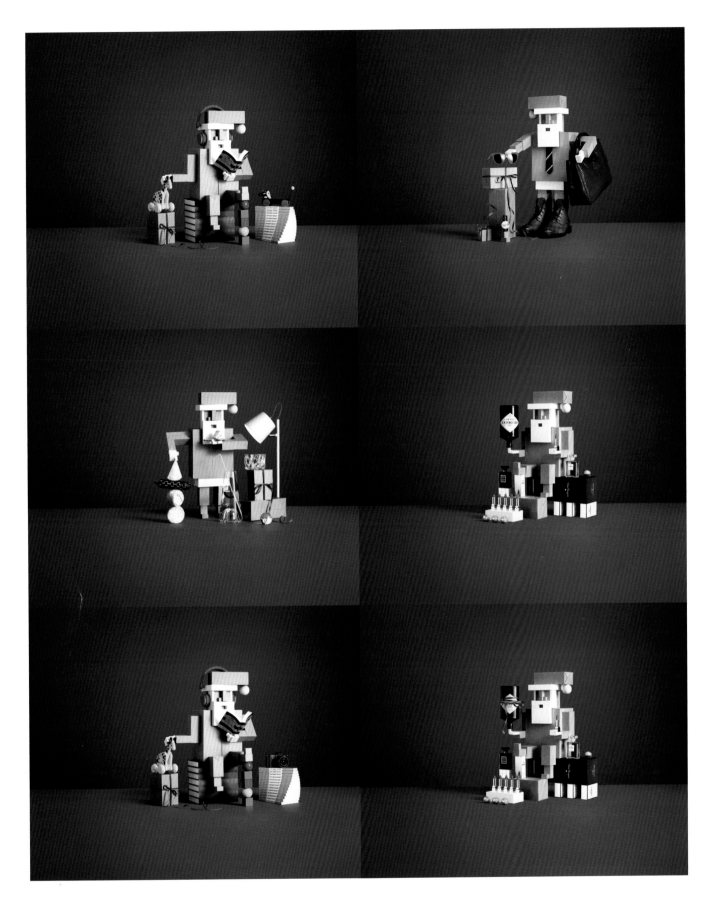

Arlanda

Ad Agency // Åkestam Holst
Styling // Camilla Krishnaswamy
Photography // Carl Kleiner

Created by photographer Carl Kleiner for Stockholm-based Arlanda International Airport's tax-free shopping area, this Christmas campaign was full of humour and creativity.

MOME Masters Night

Creative Direction // Áron Filkey, Daniel Balint,
Kristof Kiss-Benedek
Photography // Mate Moro

Flyer for Moholy-Nagy University of Art and Design
(MOME) masters night party.

Geometric Abstraction

Art Direction // Linnea Apelqvist, Ania Wawrzkowicz
Set Design & Prop Styling // Linnea Apelqvist
Photography // Ania Wawrzkowicz

The geometric shapes created a simple yet striking set, where shadows and space created depth for the products to sit in.

Personal Fakes

<u>Styling</u> // Elena Mora
<u>Photography</u> // Oliver Schwarzwald

These series of picture told a story about mystery inhabitant of this abandoned flat, showcasing clothes, products and other objects. All the environments were enlighted by paper light, just to stress the idea of magic.

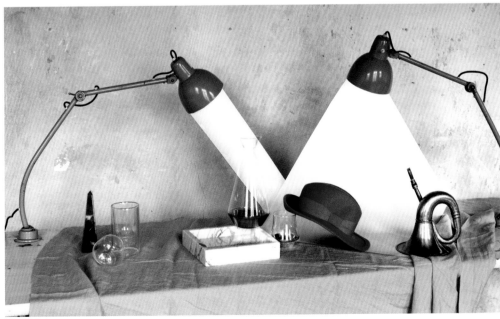

Independent Style Magazine

<u>Design</u> // Anna Lomax

Set designer Anna Lomax was commissioned by *Independent Style* magazine to create this imaginative series for the new issue.

Wonderland – The Obsession Issue

Design // Anna Lomax
Photography // Catherine Losing

Set designer Anna Lomax was commissioned by *Wonderland* magazine to create 7 alters for the 'Obsession' issue.

Parmigiani

Set Design // Jean Michel Bertin
Photography // Grégoire Alexandre

These 2 Parmigiani images were made by set designer Jean Michel Bertin and photographer Grégoire Alexandre for the Swiss watches company's magazine.

Sleek

Set Design // Jean Michel Bertin
Photography // Grégoire Alexandre

Normandy-born Grégoire Alexandre now
stationed in Paris. Cinema was his first interest,
but he became more comfortable with
photography since it gave him a greater
sense of control. He captured these beautiful
images based on his creativity.

Tea party

Pollera, vestite y andate, for C

instalacion by Puloverchito

Still Life

Creative Direction // Hernan Paganini
Art Direction // Hernan Paganini
Design // Hernan Paganini, CATALOG MAGAZINE
Photography // CATALOG MAGAZINE

Installation, sculptures and art direction for *CATALOGUE Magazine* – Summer 2010.

Catalogue

Elegidos
Catalogue

Light b

Musculosa, A.Y. Not Dead, $9

instalacion by Puloverchito

Be my guest

Camisa, Neon, $189
Florero La Mesa, 2006
Ramo de flores, gracias a Néstor Landero

Elegidos
Catalogue

In love

Bolsa, Sentina Loss, $149

instalacion by Puloverchito

Elegidos
Catalogue

Casual

Camisa hombre, A.Y. Not Dead, $239
Zapatilla, Nike, $329

instalacion by Puloverchito

Elegidos
Catalogue

Refreshed

Saco, adidas, $459

instalacion by Puloverchito

Elegidos Catalogue

Black & white

Zapatos by Las Pepas, $429

instalacion by Puloverchito

Elegidos Catalogue

Nut-brown

Buzo, A. Y. Not Dead, $189

instalacion by Puloverchito

Elegidos Catalogue

Special Coat

Campera gamuza, Doma for Catalogue
Esferas de pool de colores, La Mersa, $60 c/u

instalacion by Puloverchito

Elegidos Catalogue

Tidy

Blazer, Ayres, $428

instalacion by Puloverchito

Sol de Junio / Sun of July

<u>Creative Direction</u> // Hernan Paganini, Tomy
<u>Art Direction</u> // Hernan Paganini
<u>Photography</u> // Tomy

Installation, sculptures and art direction for *GO Magazine* – Winter 2009.

Balancing Act

<u>Creative Direction</u> // Jess Bonham, Anna Lomax
<u>Art Direction</u> // Jess Bonham, Anna Lomax
<u>Set Design</u> // Anna Lomax
<u>Photography</u> // Jess Bonham

A project began with the idea of capturing a sense of tension between the props and the products, showing the moment before a bang or a material at its elastic limit. Set designer Anna Lomax and photographer Jess Bonham also found themselves incorporating an underlying theme of housewife fetishes throughout the project. The materials and colours themselves lent themselves to a bit of suggestive connotation.

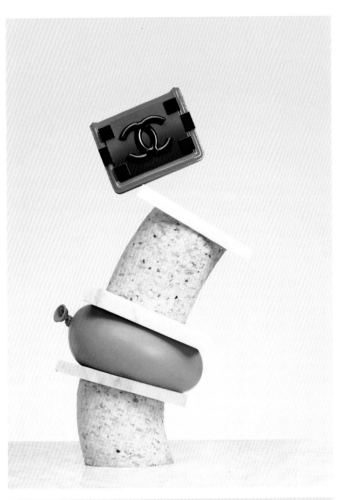

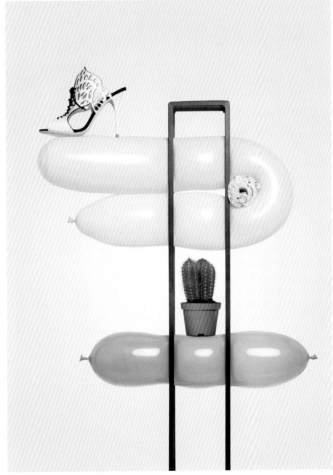

NK-stil

<u>Styling</u> // Julie von Hofsten
<u>Photography</u> // Carl Kleiner

Swedish photographer Carl Kleiner creates a witty narrative in his still life photos of everyday objects. Department store Nordiska Kompaniet commissioned him to photograph a series of pictures to showcase merchandise and relevant lifestyle articles for their own magazine *STIL*. In this project, he managed to find a clever way to tell a story.

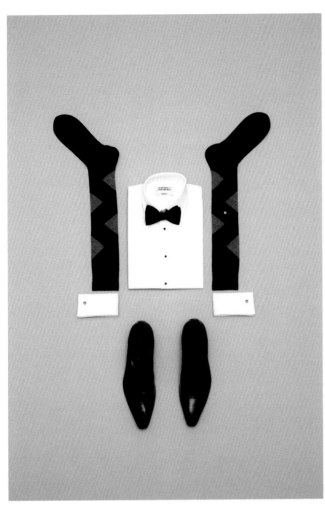

Breuninger Shoe Department

<u>Creative Direction</u> // Nicole Groezinger, Jung von Matt
<u>Art Direction</u> // Marisa Fjärem
<u>Design</u> // Marisa Fjärem
<u>Photography</u> // Serena Becker

This shoe campaign for Breuninger shoe department told the story of a queen. A queen of shoes reigned her world on a throne of shoeboxes. All props made of paper, the illustrations of her world were inspired of stories like *Alice in Wonderland* and *Cinderalla*.

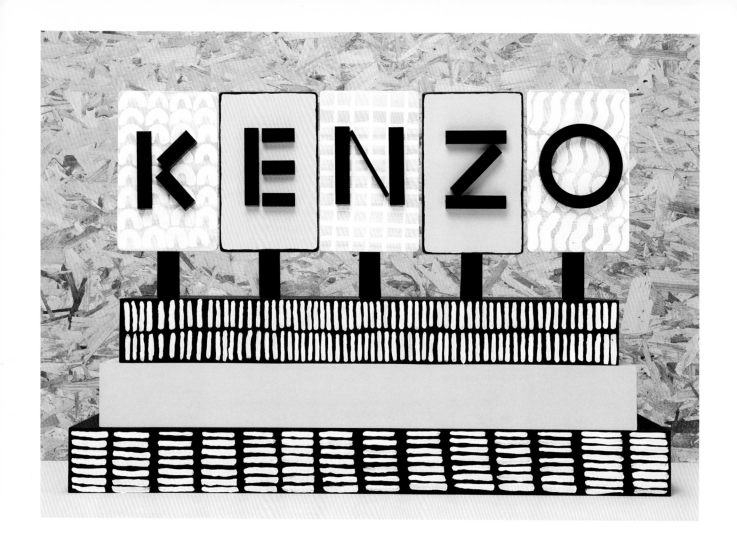

New Era Caps

<u>Creative Direction</u> // Jess Bonham, Anna Lomax
<u>Art Direction</u> // Jess Bonham, Anna Lomax
<u>Set Design</u> // Anna Lomax
<u>Photography</u> // Jess Bonham

A commission from KENZO to produce a series of images to showcase the launch of their Resort 2014 edition of caps, in collaboration with New Era. Bold patterns were used in the sets to compliment the patterns in the hats themselves.

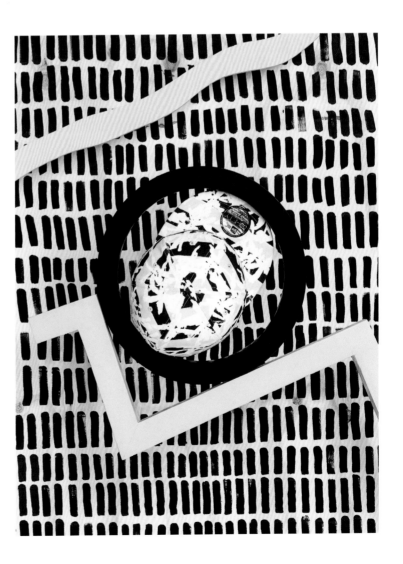

Scarfs

<u>Creative Direction</u> // Luke J Albert, Samara Tompsett
<u>Set Design</u> // Samara Tompsett
<u>Photography</u> // Luke J Albert

Photographer Luke J Albert and set designer Samara Tompsett collaborated on this personal project, playing with structural sets and colours by using scarfs as if the area of movement.

Lufthansa Exclusive Magazine

Styling // Elena Mora
Photography // Bernd Westphal

In each issue of the *Lufthansa* exclusive magazine there are different editorials about sports, fashion and products. Set designer Elena Mora was asked to show some products concerning specific sports, like sailing, golf, climbing and tennis. She created some imaginary fields of play and false perception in the viewer.

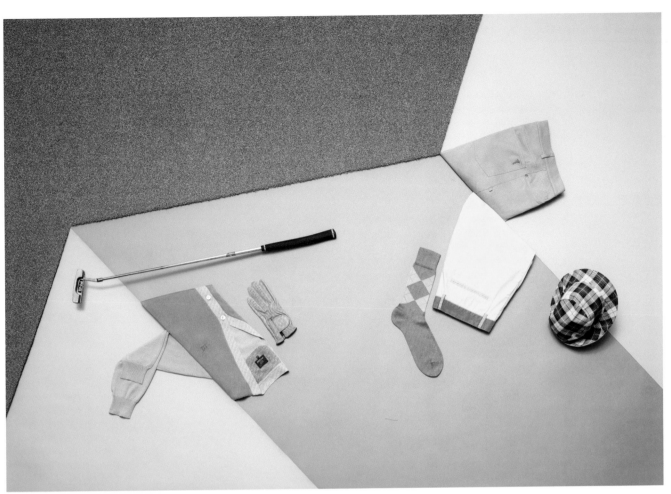

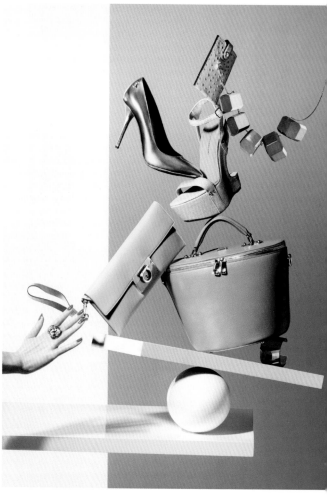

Russian Tatler Magazine – Accessories Editorial

....

<u>Art Direction</u> // Linnea Apelqvist, Chris Turner
<u>Fashion Styling</u> // Michelle Duguid
<u>Set Design & Prop Styling</u> // Linnea Apelqvist
<u>Photography</u> // Chris Turner
<u>Hand Model</u> // Nina Taylor

The monotone set had its strong lines and graphic pattern to compliment the high-end block coloured fashion accessories that the magazine had chosen. A woman's hand is never far away from causing trouble adding a sense of urgency and mischief to the story and by that introducing a playful depth to the images.

Voetstukken

Creative Direction // Caroline Brugman
Art Direction // Adrian & Gidi
Design // Adrian & Gidi
Photography // Adrian & Gidi

Adrian & Gidi was commissioned by *ELLE* magazine to shoot a 6 page still life editorial featuring women shoes. Creating abstract colourful settings combined with mixtures on which they could place the products, Adrian & Gidi just finished an installation for Bread and Butter festival (Berlin) with more than a 100 miniature buildings, so they had a wide selection of miniatures in their studio to choose from.

Hitchcock

<u>Art Direction</u> // Linnea Apelqvist
<u>Set Design & Prop Styling</u> //
Linnea Apelqvist
<u>Photography</u> // Jack Hobhouse

An interesting 2D graphic set was
created for a jewelry shoot by using
3 of Hitchcock's iconic film scenes
as a reference.

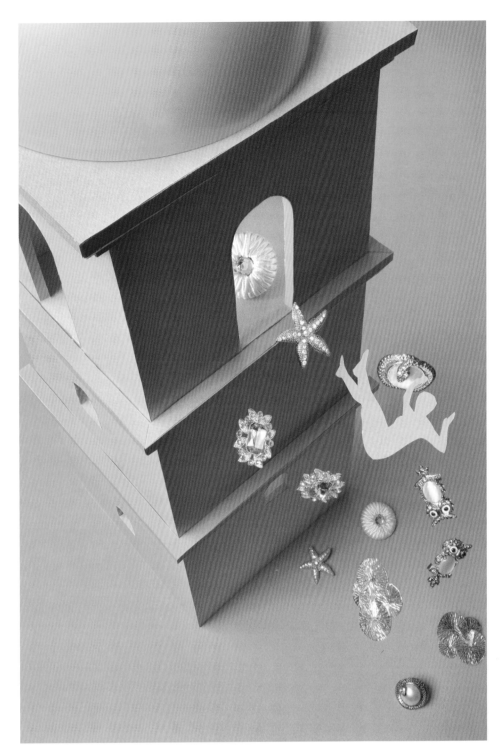

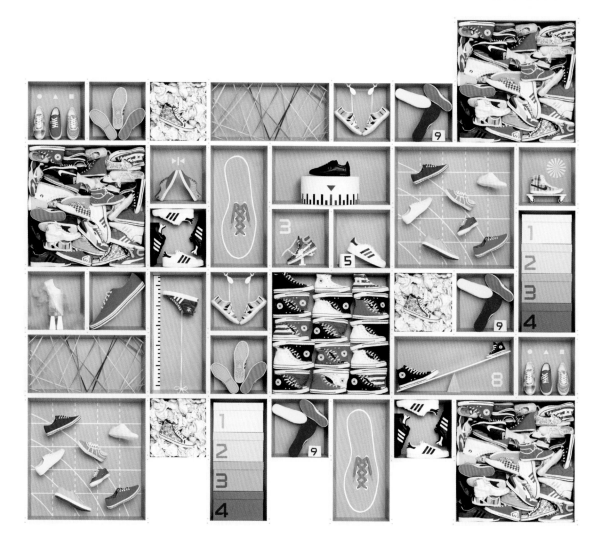

Stadium

Ad Agency // Frankenstein
Photography // Carl Kleiner

Stockholm-based photographer Carl Kleiner creates subtle, vaguely surreal compositions. His photographs show vivid colours and his own interpretations of modern ideology and culture. In this Stadium project, he created an innovative sneaker lab by using clean, clever and sharp images.

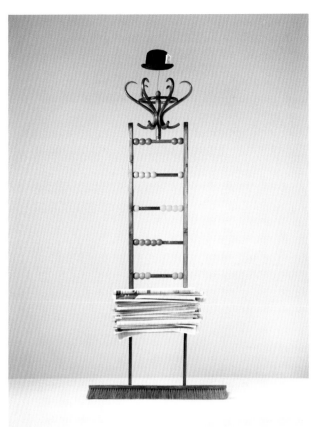

The Future of Celebrity

Creative Direction // Bianca Wendt
Art Direction // Jess Bonham, Anna Lomax
Set Design // Anna Lomax
Copywriter // Bianca Wendt
Photography // Jess Bonham

This story was commissioned for the Celebrity issue of *Viewpoint Magazine* to produce a series of images to coincide with an article about the stereotypes of the modern celebrity. The pictures illustrated the IT celebrity, the it-girl celebrity, the CGI celebrity, the intellectual celebrity, the community celebrity and the endorsed celebrity. This story in particular involved a huge amount of rigging as each set was about 9ft high!

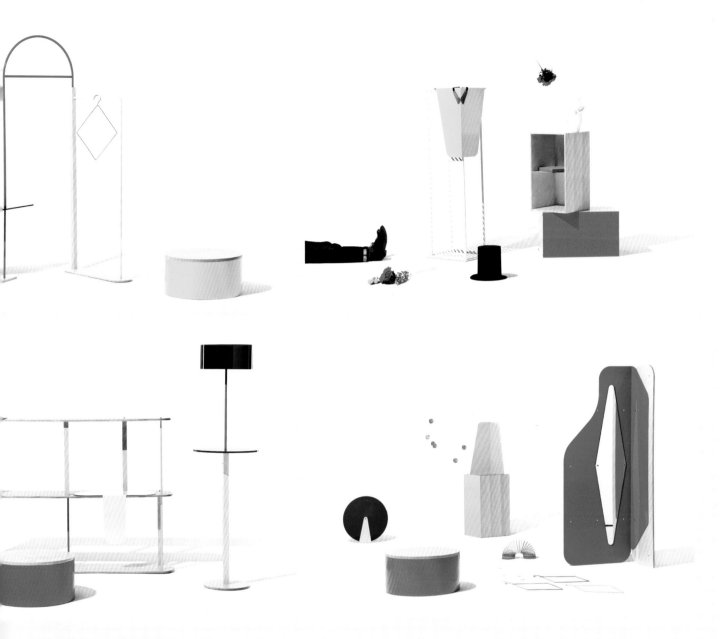

Objet Coloré

Design Agency // Fabrica
Creative Direction // Sam Baron
Art Direction // Catarina Carreiras, Dean Brown
Design // Fabrica Design Team
Photography // Fabrica

Press images for a system of store display fittings created by Fabrica to showcase United Colors of Benetton apparel and accessories.

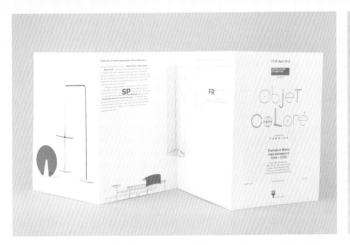

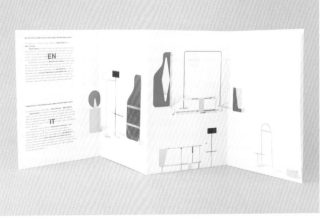

Guerlain Beauty

Set Design // Anna Lomax
Make-up // Kim Kiefer
Photography // Jess Bonham

For the outspoken issue of *Wonderland Magazine*, set designer Anna Lomax, make-up artist Kim Kiefer and photographer Jess Bonham had some fun with colour for Guerlain's new product range.

Prologue

Creative Direction // Aron Filkey, Mate Moro
Art Direction // gg-ll
Photography // Mate Moro

A collaboration between gg-ll studio, Aron Filkey and Mate Moro on the occasion of the NY Art Book Fair 2013 at MoMA PS1.

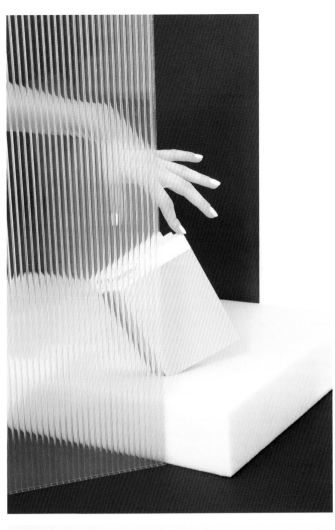

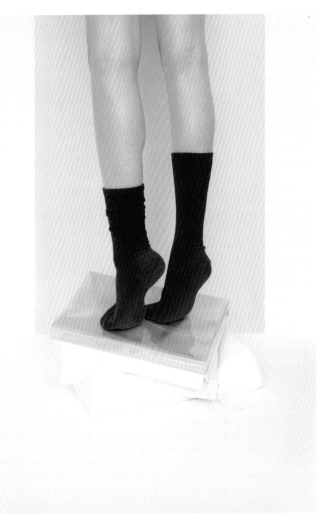

YAYOI x LV for The Room Magazine

....

Creative Direction // Mate Moro, Nora Gyenge
Art Direction // Aron Filkey
Set Design // Aron Filkey
Set Design Assistant // Richard Illes
Make-up // Laura Tegely
Hair // Mark Karolyi
Model // Rose and Barbara Tompos @ Visage
Photography // Mate Moro

Article illustration with the clothes of Yayoi Kusama
collaboration with Louis Vuitton for *The Room*
magazine issue 16.

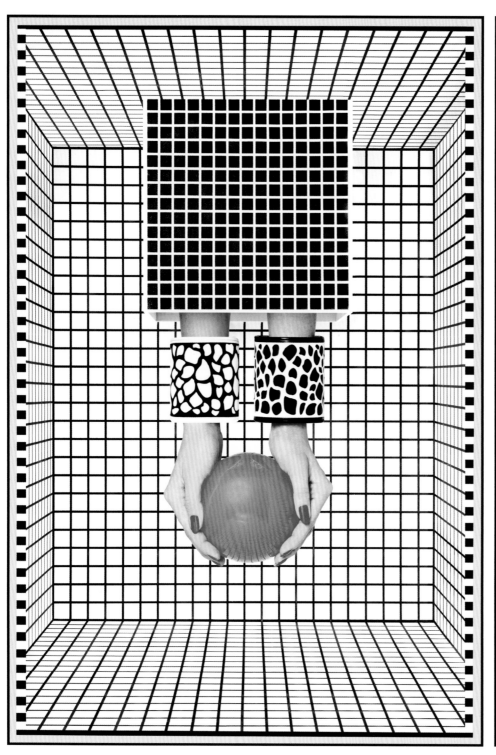

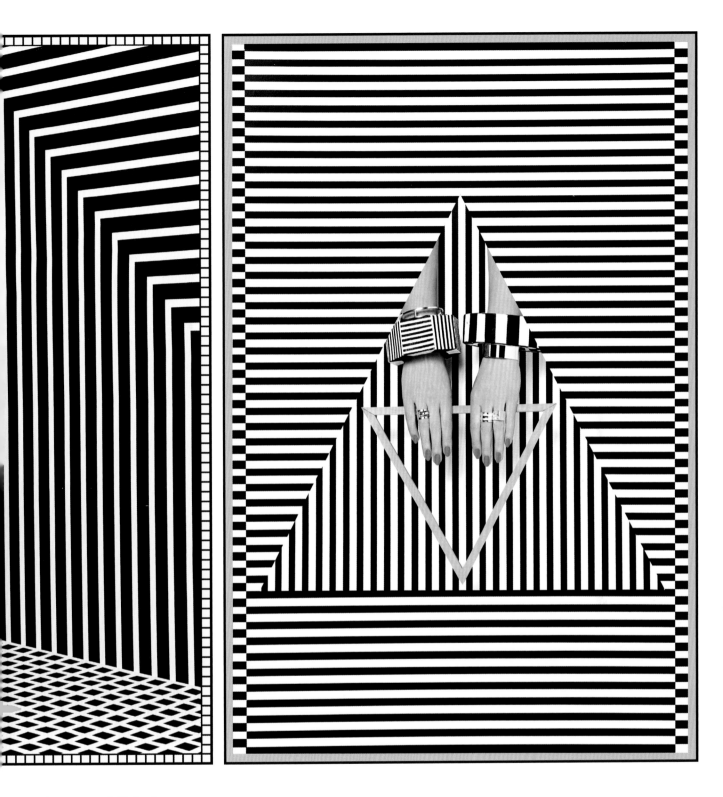

Optical Trickery

Creative Direction // Jess Bonham
Art Direction // Jess Bonham, Camille Walala
Design // Jess Bonham, Camille Walala
Styling // Camille Walala
Model Maker // Jess Bonham, Camille Walala
Photography // Jess Bonham

Textile designer and pattern connoisseur Camille Walala and photographer Jess Bonham had long been talking about doing a project together. In this project, the photographer wanted to explore how they could bring her two-dimensional imagery into a three dimensional world. There was a play on the juxtaposition between the real and the surreal to bring something tangible into that world, such as legs and arms.

Odd Pears Campaign

Creative Direction // Leta Sobierajski

The theme of the Odd Pears Spring Collaboration was surrealism. Four engaging portraits which would compliment each other as a set were created. The main visual components were the socks, which were different for each image, so the figure's identity was to be determined by its palette. The images began as sketches before being composed on set with matching props, consisting of hand-painted fruits, balloons, and furniture. Once each "figure" was developed, the photographs were matched up to create each final composition. None of the elements were computer-generated, as a main goal was to capture everything in camera and preserve as much authenticity as possible.

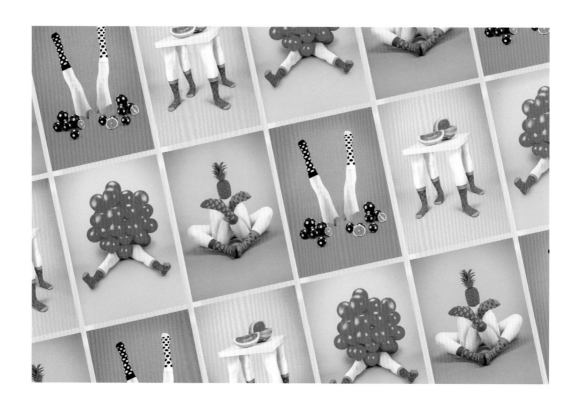

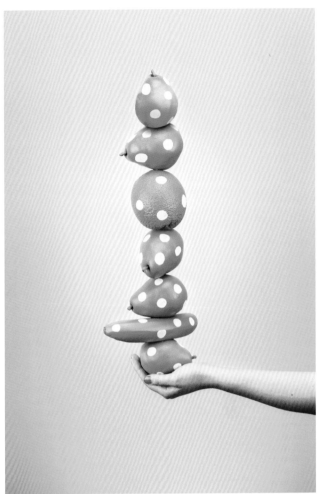

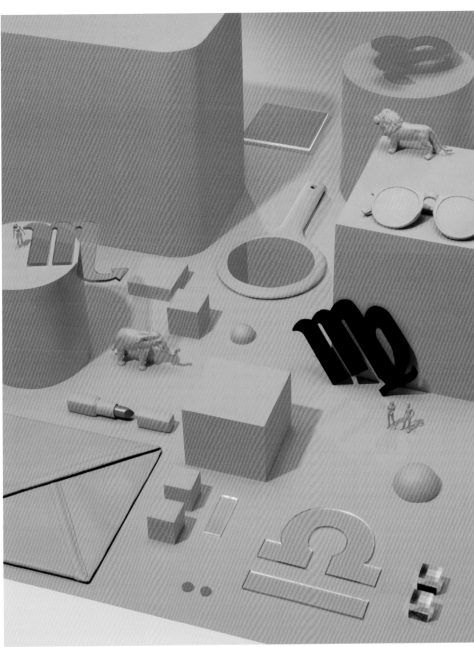

Horoscopes 2014

<u>Creative Direction</u> // Caroline Brugman
<u>Art Direction</u> // Adrian & Gidi
<u>Set Design</u> // Adrian & Gidi
<u>Photography</u> // Adrian & Gidi

Adrian & Gidi was commissioned by *ELLE* magazine to shoot their monthly horoscope illustrations. The final results were 3 pictures, each containing 4 horoscope images which can be cropped out of the total image.

Wallpaper*

Set Design // Elena Mora
Styling // Elena Mora
Photography // Qiu Yang

Set designer Elena Mora was asked by *Wallpaper** magazine to think about 4 images that could show the spirit and mood of important design events. They took the 4 main ones, Paris Maison et Object, Milano Salone del Mobile, London Design Week and Miami Art Basel. Each picture showed some design products related to the city, placed on stereotyped buildings. Also, there were elements and tools of the creative process behind design: sketches, pencils rulers, etc.

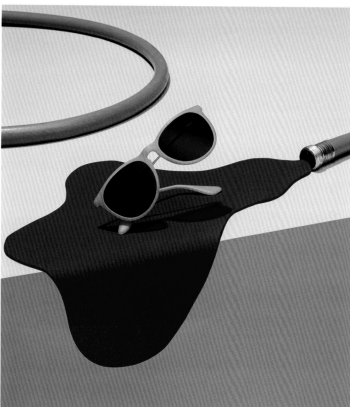
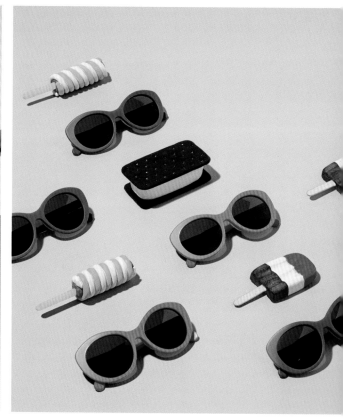

BonLook Summer 2014 Campagin

<u>Creative Direction</u> // Nik Mirus, Oliver Stenberg (@L'ELOI)
<u>Art Direction</u> // Tania Fugulin
<u>Set Design</u> // Oliver Stenberg
<u>Photography</u> // Nik Mirus (@L'ELOI)

The project was inspired by bright, playful surrealism mixed with summer fun. Every image was to tell a different story, but all tie into the same colourful world. To create this world, classic summer objects were put on vivid colour palettes with the client's perfectly fitted sunglasses.

Museum of Broken Relationships

....

<u>Creative Direction</u> // Caroline Brugman
<u>Art Direction</u> // Adrian & Gidi
<u>Set Design</u> // Adrian & Gidi
<u>Photography</u> // Adrian & Gidi

Adrian & Gidi was commissioned by *Elle* magazine to shoot photo illustration to accompany an article about 'The Museum of Broken Relationships.' They received sentimental artifacts from famous Dutch people that reminded them of past relationships and then photographed the object together with a broken heart made of foam.

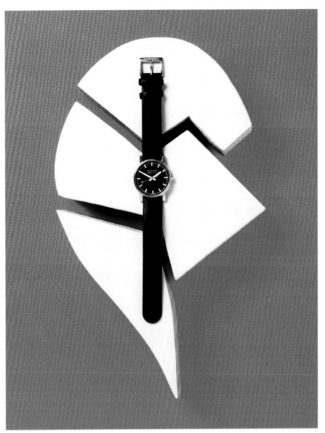

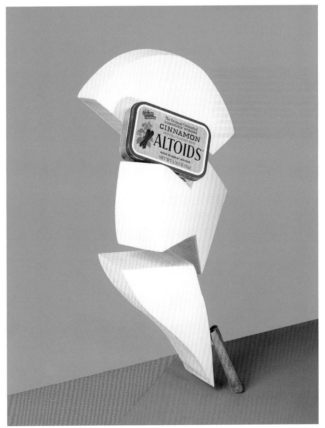

Ode To Ellen Gallagher

Creative Direction // Jess Bonham, Anna Lomax
Art Direction // Jess Bonham, Anna Lomax
Set Design // Anna Lomax
Copywriter // Holly Hay
Photography // Jess Bonham

The brief was to produce visuals to coincide with the opening of the Ellen Gallagher's retrospective at the Tate Modern. Avoiding entering too much into the very personal and political ideals of Ellen Gallagher's work, set designer Anna Lomax and photographer Jess Bonham drew from her colour pallette and the main imagery of hair to build up the scenes.

Sunglasses

Art Direction // James Lambert
Illustration // James Lambert
Set Design // Alexandra Leavey
Photography // Victoria Ling

This was a personal project, combining layering of colour and texture in camera and in post production. The glasses were shot through sheets of glass layered with paint and objects, creating a depth of field and natural feel and then art worked with additional elements in post.

Inevitable fin de año en el bosque

<u>Creative Direction</u> // M.Laura Benavente (AKA mililitros)
<u>Art Direction</u> // M.Laura Benavente
<u>Design</u> // El Estudio™
<u>Set Design</u> // M.Laura Benavente
<u>Photography</u> // M.Laura Benavente

Poster for a new year's eve party in Tenerife, Canary Islands. The Party concept was the artificial forest, and the visuals, decoration and installation were made under the concept "inevitable fin de año en el bosque" that means "inevitable new year's eve at the forest" in English.

Curious Breakfast

<u>Art Direction</u> // Alexis Facca
<u>Photography</u> // Fanette Guilloud

This paper breakfast was achieved by two French artists Alexis Facca and Fanette Guilloud, creating a typical French and American breakfast. The piece of art was made as participation for a competition named Your Curious Story.

Wycinanka

<u>Styling</u> // Aliki Kirmitsi
<u>Photography</u> // Ania Wawrzkowicz

Wycinanka is a Polish folk art of papercutting and layering. To celebrate the 10th year anniversary of *Elle Deco Poland*, set designer Aliki Kirmitsi and photographer Ania Wawrzkowicz were commissioned to produce a series of images. They drew inspiration from this lovely folk art which captured Poland's creative beat. Using the Wycinanka technique and kitchen products, they created forms that decorated *Elle Deco*'s celebratory pages.

SCHOTT Ceran®

Creative Direction // Dana Kreidt
Art Direction // Ollanski, Cris Wiegandt
Model Maker // Ollanski, Cris Wiegandt,
Elfriede, La Mirasola
Copywriter // Dana Kreidt
Photography // Felipe Campos,
Rod Di Sciascio,
Carolin Wimmer

The advertising agency Shanghai Berlin
commissioned Ollanski and Cris Wiegandt
to create four explanation movies about
the product SCHOTT Ceran®. All the objects
were entirely made out of paper.

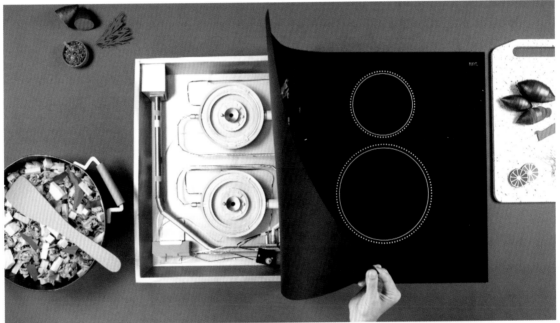

IKEA Woonbeurs

<u>Art Direction</u> // Jessica Guerrero,
                           Koen Hogewoning
<u>Styling</u> // Bibi Silver Funcke
<u>Photography</u> // Wendy van Santen

These images were created for IKEA for the annual Woonbeurs (interior fair). Large compositions were created on the floor, using IKEA kitchen related products. Each image symbolized a different type/ style of kitchen, such as a playful kitchen for families and a world kitchen.

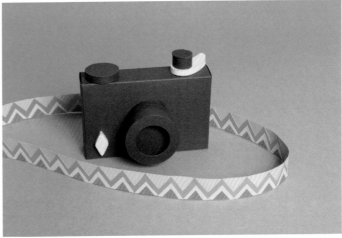

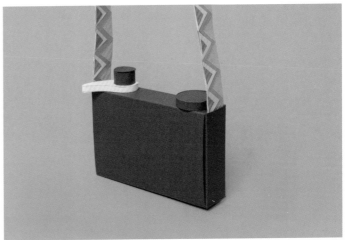

Master Application

<u>Design</u> // Carolin Wanitzek
<u>Photography</u> // Carolin Wanitzek

This cover illustration was part of the Master Application and personified who Carolin Wanitzek is.

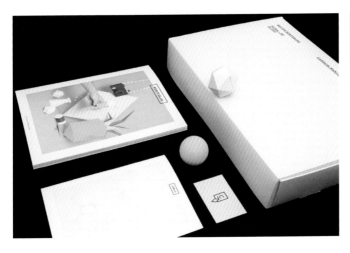

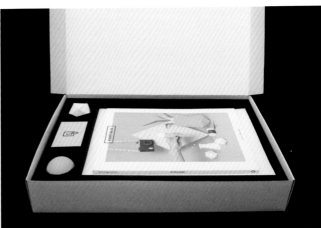

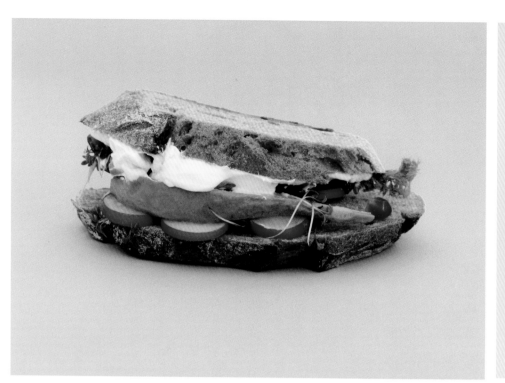

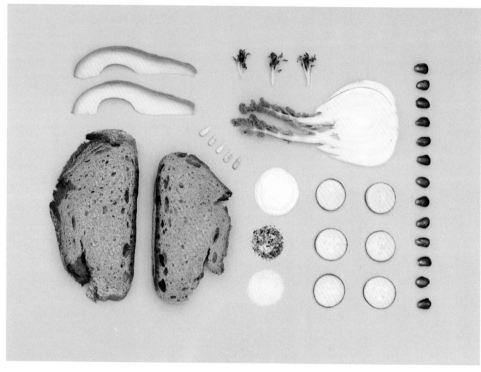

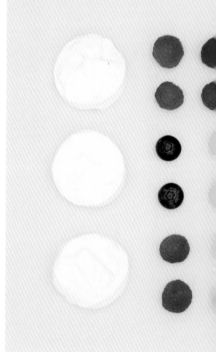

Goldentree

<u>Design</u> // Carolin Wanitzek, Dennis Adelmann
<u>Photography</u> // Carolin Wanitzek,
Dennis Adelmann

Goldentree was a project for a concept store in Frankfurt, Germany. The concept store is a blend of cloths, furniture, vintage stuff, food and beverage. Carolin Wanitzek and Dennis Adelmann created a whole corporate identity. The installations for the food department showed the ingredients of the sandwich in a graphical way.

IBM: Chef Watson

Art Direction // Sue Murphy
Design // Leta Sobierajski

Advertising agency Ogilvy & Mather commissioned Leta Sobierajski to develop the imagery for the launch of IBM's Chef Watson app, where cognitive computing helps you discover recipes that never existed before. They worked with the craziest combinations they could think of, keeping the imagery in a four-colour primary colour palette. The header image covered IBM's Facebook and Twitter headers, while the three animated gifs were released a day apart to help introduce the app through Tumblr, Twitter, and Facebook alike. Captions created prompts for users, such as "What's your spin on bacon & dragon fruit?" and "3 eggs. 2 pinches of coriander. 1 cognitive system." It was a fun, messy, and somewhat stinky project that left them sticky and smelling like ketchup.

Mercado Central Campaign

<u>Creative Direction</u> // Club de Esgrima, M.Laura Benavente
<u>Art Direction</u> // Club de Esgrima, M.Laura Benavente
<u>Design</u> // Club de Esgrima, M.Laura Benavente
<u>Set Design</u> // M.Laura Benavente
<u>Copywriter</u> // M.Laura Benavente
<u>Photography</u> // M.Laura Benavente

In this communication campaign, the Central Market wanted to attract young audiences. The idea was to conduct a series of pieces of cardboard that compiled some of the market products differently so that they would be attractive to the eyes. All items were handmade with brightly coloured backgrounds to achieve the desired contrast in photographs.

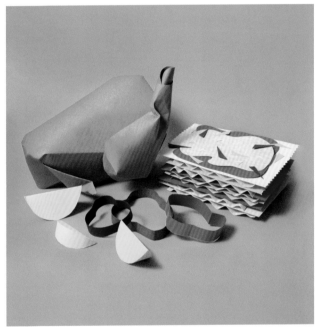

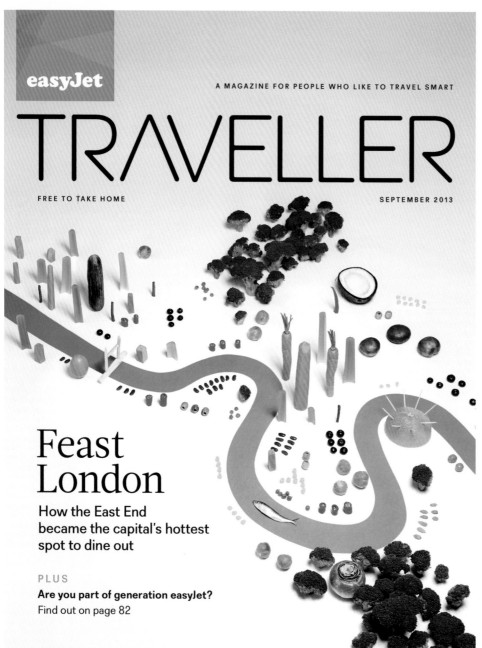

easyJet

A MAGAZINE FOR PEOPLE WHO LIKE TO TRAVEL SMART

TRAVELLER

FREE TO TAKE HOME

SEPTEMBER 2013

Feast London

How the East End
became the capital's hottest
spot to dine out

PLUS

Are you part of generation easyJet?
Find out on page 82

East End Eats

<u>Creative Direction</u> // Mat Wiggins
<u>Design</u> // Kyle Bean
<u>Illustration</u> // Kyle Bean
<u>Photography</u> // Catherine Losing

A cover image created for *easyJets Traveller* magazine highlighting new exciting restaurants that have opened in the Capitals East End. The image depicted a graphic map of the East End of London constructed from different ingredients. Kyle Bean constructed the map which was then photographed by Catherine Losing.

Social Enterprise – Willem & Drees

Art Direction // Fabian Sapthu
Styling // Bibi Sliver Funcke
Photography // Wendy van Santen

Willem & Drees brings locally produced fruits and vegetables from the farmlands to the city. The image shows an urban skyline. The grey buildings are actually just spray painted supermarket products. They stand for boring and drab industrial mass produced foods. Colourful paths cut through the city. On them, armies of fresh produce enter the city. Like the farmers from the surrounding lands they bring colour back to the city.

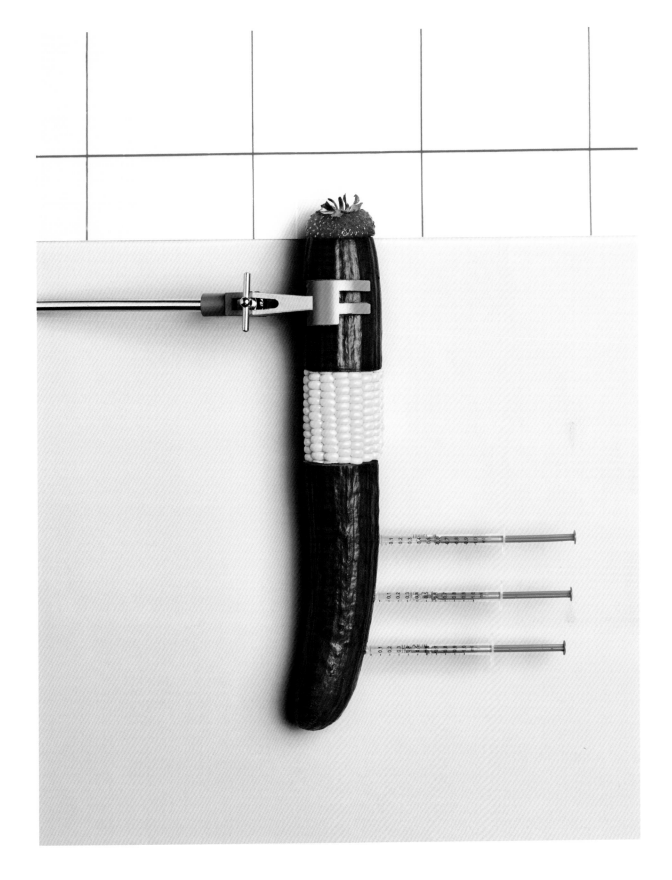

Das Datan Dinner

<u>Creative Direction</u> // Markus Rindermann
<u>Art Direction</u> // Jess Bonham, Jamie Julian-Brown
<u>Design</u> // Jess Bonham, Jamie Julian-Brown
<u>Styling</u> // Jamie Julien-Brown
<u>Copywriter</u> // Alisa Evokimov
<u>Photography</u> // Jess Bonham

The images were created to coincide with an article about 'Food Printing,' a diet that relies on software to provide unexpected combinations of food pairs, designed to optimise nutrition for a specific individual's needs.

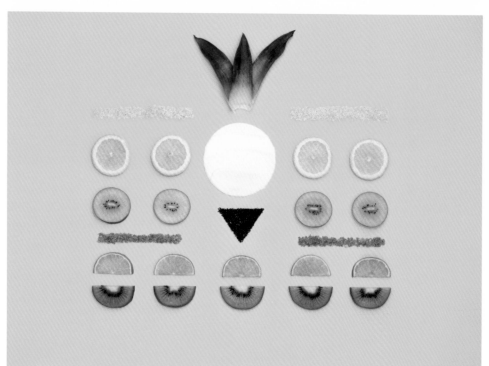

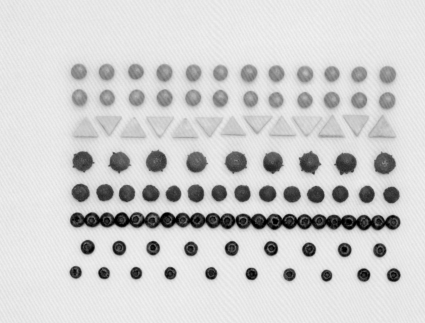

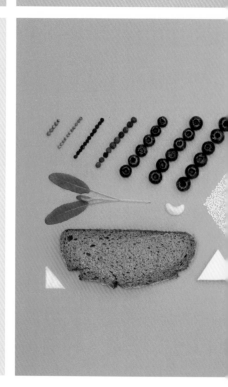

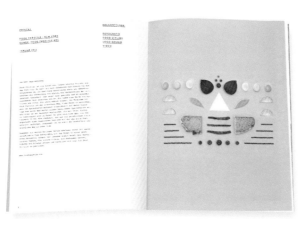

Food Throttle

Design // Carolin Wanitzek, Dennis Adelmann
Photography // Carolin Wanitzek, Dennis Adelmann

Food Throttle is a startup from New York City. It aims to be a comprehensive dieting solution for individuals looking to meet certain dietary goals. Six different food images were created to show the food in a way of a graphical arrangement. Two arranging videos that show the creation process and four videos that show rotating vegetables, fruits and herbs were made as well.

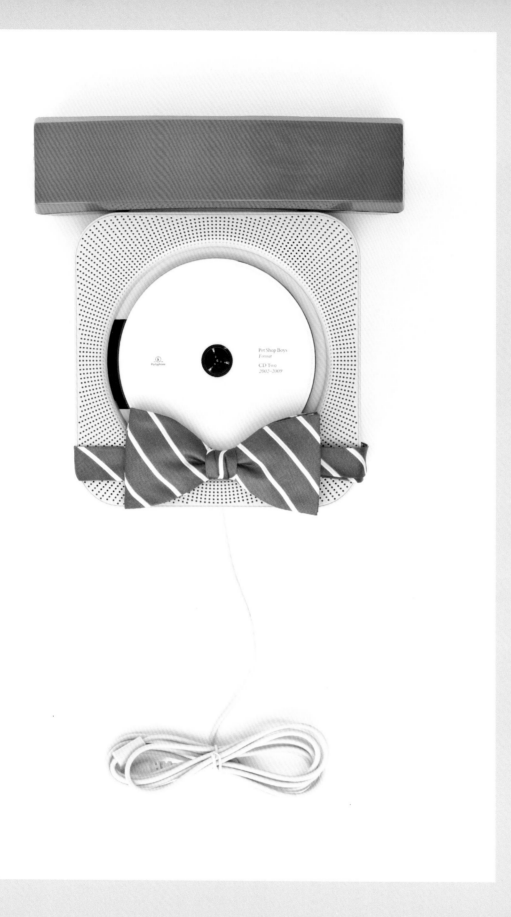

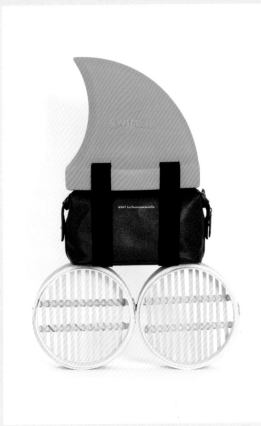

Causación Formativa

Art Direction // Roberto Ruiz
Publishing // B-guided Magazine nº 51
Photography // Roberto Ruiz

Selection of housewares and daily accessories with relational games created new formal structures, which challenged usability of objects with formalist games.

#50
INVIERNO / WINTER
2012

MODA, ARTE, DISEÑO,
ARQUITECTURA,
GASTRONOMÍA, MÚSICA,
ENTRETENIMIENTO

FASHION, ART, DESIGN,
ARCHITECTURE,
GASTRONOMY, MUSIC,
ENTERTAINMENT

BARCELONA

b-guided >

ESPAÑA: 5 EUROS

#51
PRIMAVERA 2012
SPRING 2012

MODA, ARTE, DISEÑO,
ARQUITECTURA,
GASTRONOMÍA, MÚSICA,
ENTRETENIMIENTO

FASHION, ART, DESIGN,
ARCHITECTURE,
GASTRONOMY, MUSIC,
ENTERTAINMENT

BARCELONA

b-guided >

ESPAÑA/SPAIN: 5 EUR.

#52
VERANO 2012
SUMMER 2012

FASHION, ART, DESIGN,
ARCHITECTURE,
GASTRONOMY, MUSIC,
ENTERTAINMENT

MODA, ARTE, DISEÑO,
ARQUITECTURA,
GASTRONOMÍA, MÚSICA,
ENTRETENIMIENTO

BARCELONA

b-guided >

ESPAÑA/SPAIN: 5 EUR.

#53
OTOÑO-INVIERNO 2012
AUTUMN-WINTER 2012

MODA, ARTE, DISEÑO,
ARQUITECTURA,
GASTRONOMÍA, MÚSICA,
ENTRETENIMIENTO

FASHION, ART, DESIGN,
ARCHITECTURE,
GASTRONOMY, MUSIC,
ENTERTAINMENT

BARCELONA

b-guided >

ESPAÑA/SPAIN: 5 EUR.

Desktop Flora and Fauna

Art Direction // Roberto Ruiz
Publishing // B-guided Magazine nº 57
Photography // Roberto Ruiz

The floral theme was the link in this still life work. Natural flowers were accompanied by selected objects and papers that depicted the background.

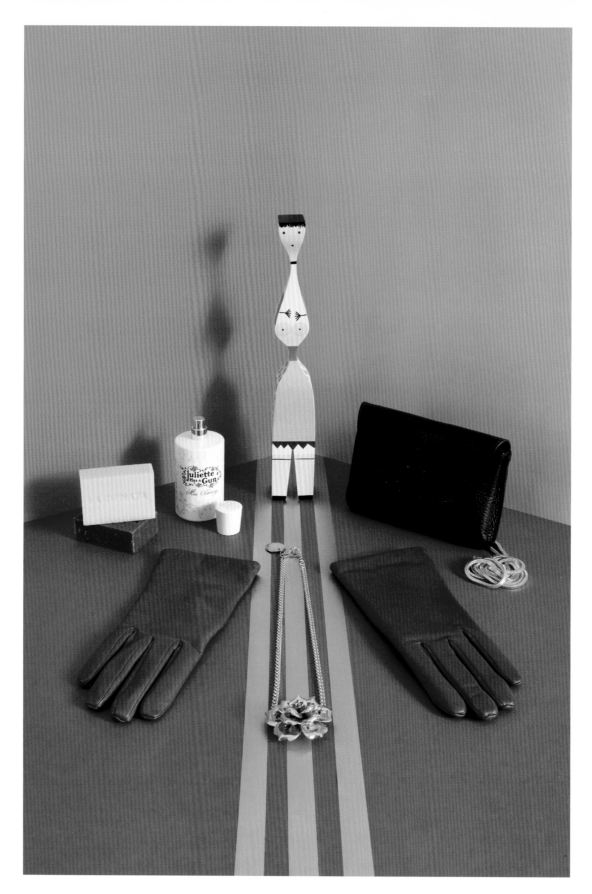

Wrapping Lines

....

Art Direction // Roberto Ruiz
Publishing // B-guided Magazine nº 56
Photography // Roberto Ruiz

This editorial work was created for *B-guided* Christmas issue of the magazine. Based on the idea of showing prospective gifts, the object selections were made to organise the Christmas table. Colour plans were combined with packing tape gifts, looking for connections based on themes, colours and formal structures.

Play

Art Direction // Roberto Ruiz
Publishing // B-guided Magazine nº 54
Photography // Roberto Ruiz

Play was a visual work of experimentation and playing with plans, shapes and colours. The objects related to each other based on composing still life themes with different visual plans, shades and colours.

Nido Wish Case

<u>Art Direction</u> // Nina Bannayer (Nido)
<u>Design</u> // Carolin Wanitzek
<u>Styling</u> // Carolin Wanitzek
<u>Photography</u> // Carolin Wanitzek,
                 Diane Vincent (Magazine Photography)

German family magazine *Nido* commissioned Carolin Wanitzek to make a case full of wishes for the Christmas special issue. This case should give families the motivation to visualize their wishes, whether to have more time to stay with your family or to wish a dinosaur as a birthday present – everything is possible!

Table and Desk

<u>Creative Direction</u> // Luke J Albert, Alice King
<u>Set Design</u> // Alice King
<u>Photography</u> // Luke J Albert

Photographer Luke J Albert and set designer Alice King collaborated on this self-initiated project, playing with directional light as a colour source. Everything was shot through camera as it was.

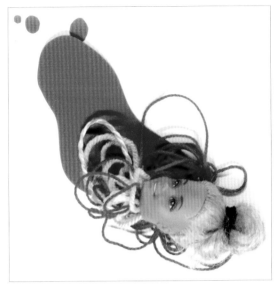

Zombieland

Design // Carolin Wanitzek
Photography // Carolin Wanitzek

This crazy movie poster was the collaborative result
of Carolin Wanitzek and two German designers from
Hamburg, Falko Ohlmer and Ole Utikal. The task was to
create a typographic movie poster.

24

Photo illustration project developed solely in camera with paper, wood, paint, and fishing wire. 24 was a short series in which two wooden hands clinked glasses in celebration and floated in faux-surreal settings.

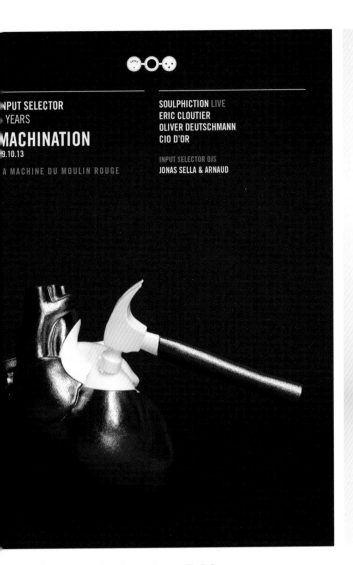

Input Selector 5 Years

Design // Jonas Sellami

For its 5 years of existence, the French musical webzine Input Selector decided to organise 3 parties between Nantes and Paris. Each artwork was made in agreement with the party mood, from cold and dark techno to more groovy and coloured house music.

A Story of Ice Cream Cones, Surgical Gloves and Other Stuff

....

<u>Art Direction</u> // Hans Bolleurs
<u>Styling</u> // Bibi Silver Funcke
<u>Photography</u> // Wendy van Santen

For this series photographer Wendy van Santen decided to make still compositions and little abstract stories, with all the unused props lying around in her studio. Together with the stylist and art director, they got all the items out and started to improvise images. Some photos in the series resembled surreal landscapes, while others hinted at traditional still lifes. The bubblegum colours and graphic elements tied different items together. Each object told its own story.

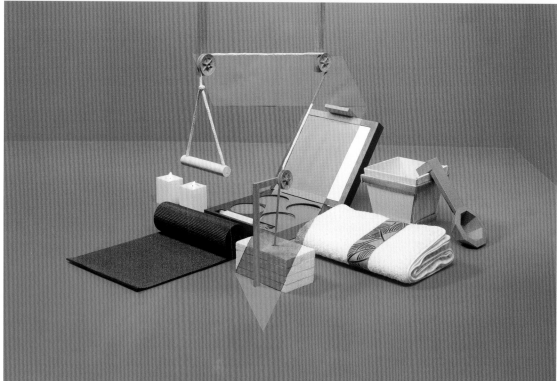

7TV Rebranding

Creative Direction // Greg Barth
Art Direction // Vanda Daftari,
                    Capucine Labarthe
Set Direction // Sylvain Lavoie

The rebranding was intended to strengthen 7TV's new image as a Do-it yourself channel. One that promotes health, education, and general knowledge about how to better yourself.

The minimal look was chosen to evoke a certain Zen and meditative state of mind, playing on the ambiguity of full versus empty spaces. It also allowed us to derive the branding into various moods, depending on the channel's topics (Travel, Construction / Renovation, Cinema, Changing Yourself, Relationships), giving the Identity a changing character, colour and feel.

The concept was to highlight that through an organised and smart assembly. You can improve your life, making all the pieces of the puzzle fit perfectly together. To emphasize an honest and human approach, all on-screen elements were made and animated by hand.

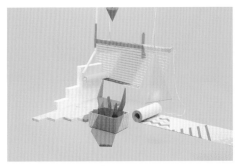

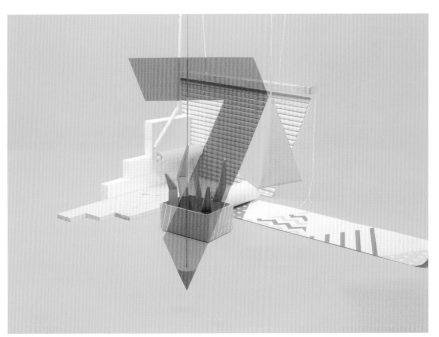

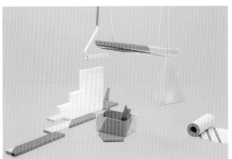

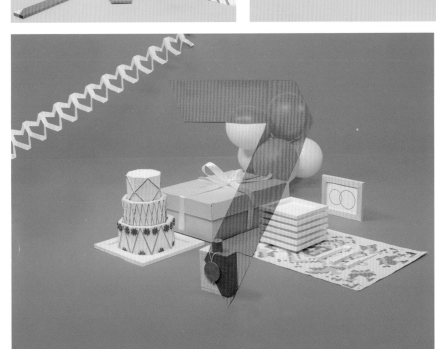

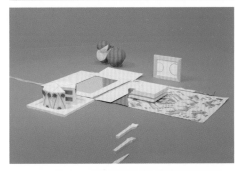

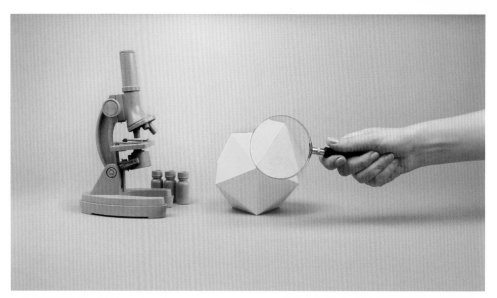

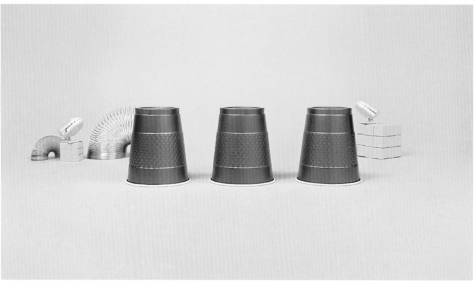

Applications

Creative Direction // Leta Sobierajski
Audio // O Sole Mio by Luciano Pavarotti
Hand Model // Laura Benack, Rachel Fuller,
          Erin Goldberger, Marta Massague

Personal animation project illustrating the build up and deconstruction of a series of events featuring a pleasant colour palette. The entire production was shot in camera with every day objects. The fish Newton passed away in the summer 2012 after living a happy and healthy life.

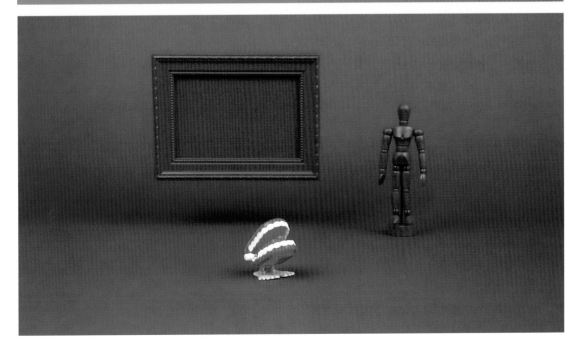

MARS T
Undress Me EP
⬢
Incl. Joris Delacroix remix

Timid Records

Design // Jonas Sellami

Timid Records is a French electronic music label. The aim of this project was to play around the extruded timid logo depending on the title, the musical direction of the EP, the flyer or a marking event.

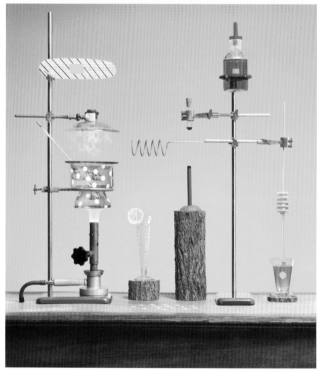

Measures of Quality

Creative Direction // Jess Bonham,
Jamie Julian-Brown
Art Direction // Jess Bonham,
Jamie Julian-Brown
Set Design // Jamie Julien-Brown
Copywriter // Dave Lane, Marina Tweed
Photography // Jess Bonham

Jess Bonham shared a studio with Jamie Julian-Brown, who at the time had been collecting some amazing pieces of old scientific glassware on his shelves. Jess suggested they should collaborate on a still life shoot, using Jamie's glassware as a starting point. They pitched the idea of a scientific food story to *The Gourmand* and suggested a cocktail story for their next issue which they were very happy to go with! They invited the mixologist Ryan Chetiyawardana to advise them on how best to construct the story and together they decided on taking a classic cocktail of each of the five main cocktail families and display a breakdown of their contents to the exact ratio. These cocktails and the families to which they belong broke down in their story as: The Hot Toddy- Punches, the Whiskey Sour- Sours, the Sea Breeze- Highball, the Martini- Cocktail and the Margarita- Daisy. They wanted to capture a sense of the character of each cocktail in the colours and shapes within the compositions, e.g. the shapes of the scientific glassware mirrored the type of glass that each cocktail would be served in, ect.

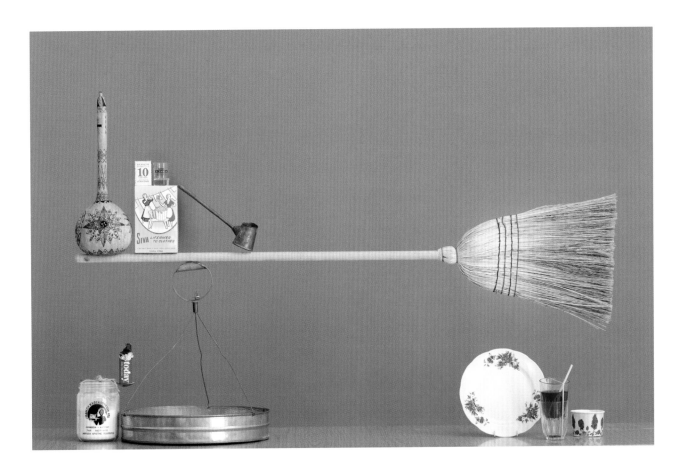

Cyprus Cult

Styling // Aliki Kirmitsi
Photography // Antonis Farmakas

Avant Garde Press is an alternative and creative publication in Cyprus that focuses on cultural subjects. This set was an editorial story that tapped into the true essence of being a Cypriot, reflected through items which best construct the memories of a 'true' local. Cyprus Cult was shot in Cyprus with Cypriot photographer Antonis Farmakas; Aliki Kirmitsi created a raw simple sculpture that depicts the islanders' roots and persona.

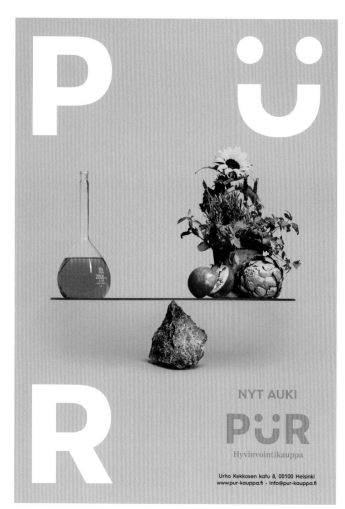

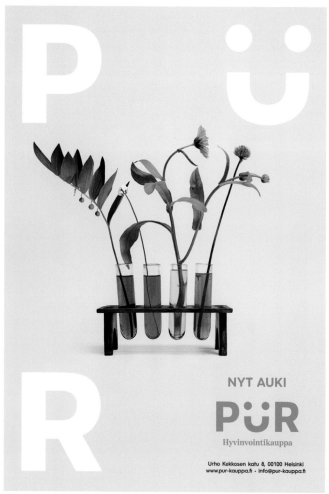

PUR

Design Agency // Bond Creative Agency
Creative Direction // Arttu Salovaara
Design // Aleksi Hautamäki, Toni Hurme,
        Janne Norokytö, Annika Peltoniemi,
        Jesper Bange, Lawrence Dorrington

PUR is a new generation of wellness shops in Helsinki, bringing various aspects of healthy living together under one roof. Design agency Bond created a complete branding concept that covered everything from the brand identity to the shop design, website, photography, advertising and marketing collaterals. All this helps PUR to communicate its message of holistic wellbeing in an appealing, fun and informative way.

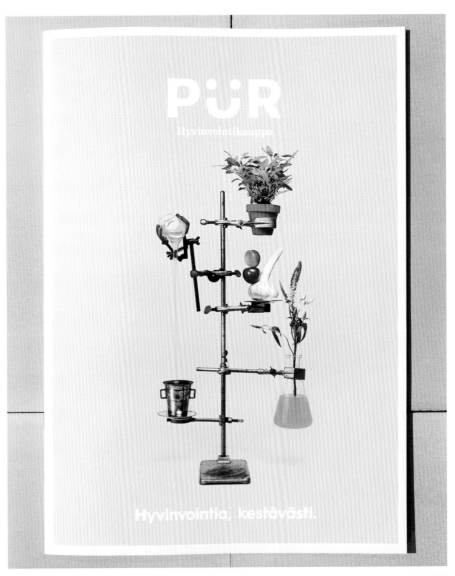

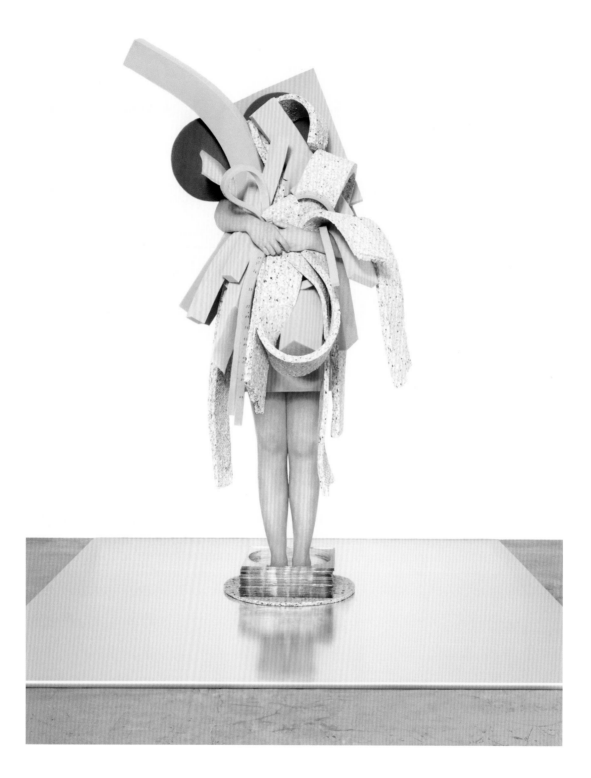

Body Builder

Creative Direction // Jess Bonham
Art Direction // Jess Bonham, Anna Lomax
Set Design // Anna Lomax
Photography // Jess Bonham

This project explored ways in which we could use the body as a structural support upon which we could build upon. The materials used were pretty extreme in size and layers, so that the limbs you can see are the only indication of what was happening in the scene.

The Illusions Issue, Little Burgundy Magazine

<u>Design</u> // Greg Barth
<u>Photography</u> // Greg Barth

Greg Barth was invited by Aldo's Little Burgundy stores to create a cover and images for their magazine's "Illusions" issue. All effects you see on the pictures were done using "in-camera" techniques, and Photoshop was only used to clean up the images.

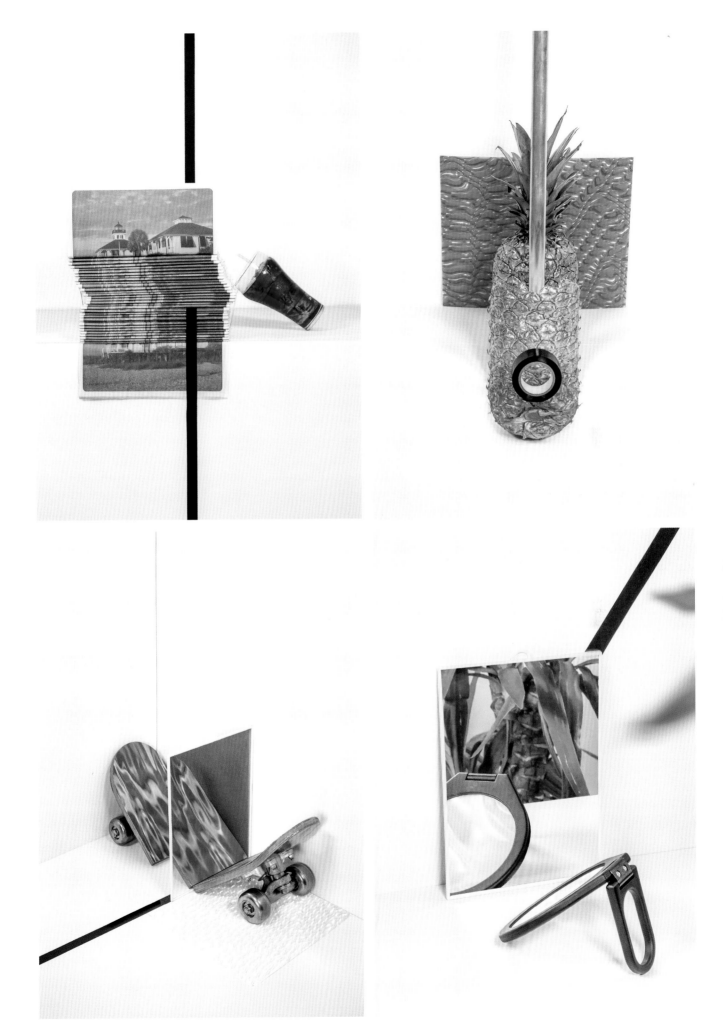

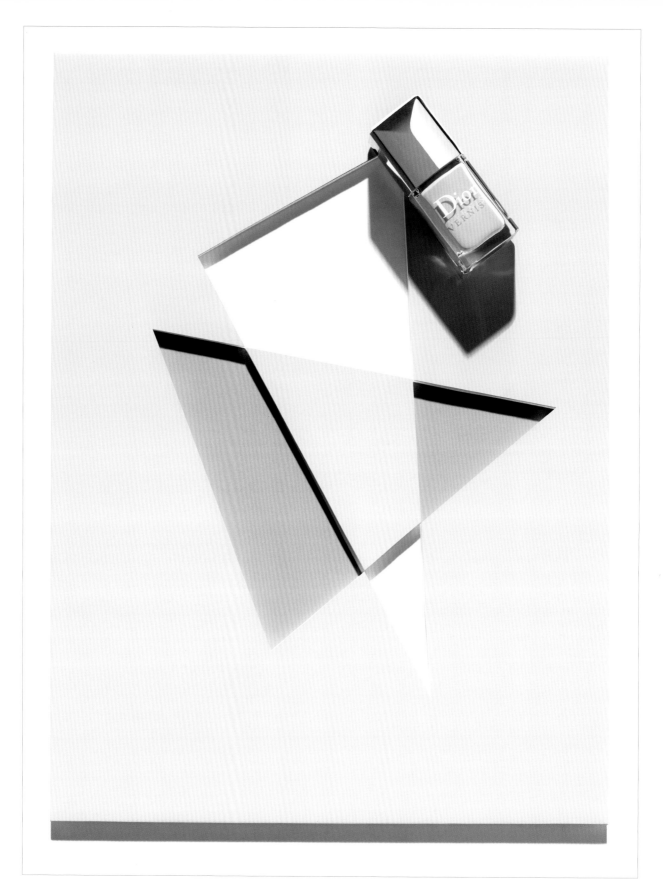

Albers

__Design__ // Ben Pogue
__Photography__ // Ben Pogue

This project was conceived, fabricated and executed by photographer Ben Pogue for his personal work. Each photograph represented a page taken from *Interaction of Color* by Josef Albers. Pogue built the set to scale and used the same Colour Aid materials that Albers himself taught with. Then he added the cosmetics to give the story a more playful feel, reflecting on the way colour is used in that industry as well.

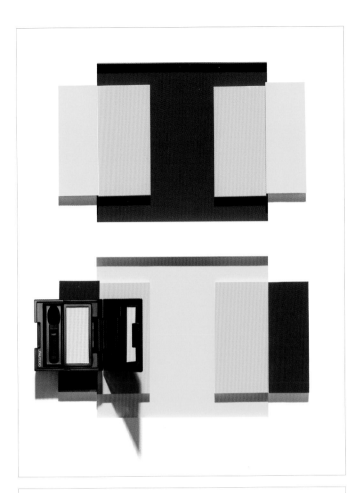

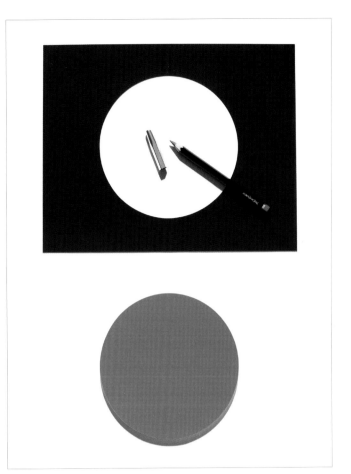

Intersport

Ad Agency // Made to Order
Set Design // Evelina Kleiner
Photography // Carl Kleiner

Sports retailer Intersport commissioned Swedish photographer Carl Kleiner to create a small campaign for the festive season. It featured a few of our favorite things and completed with badminton birdies, baseballs, skate decks, boxing gloves, etc.

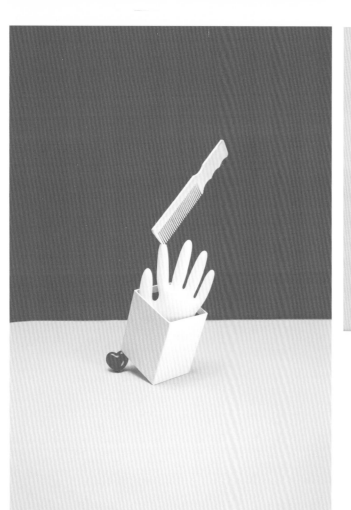

Orkeny Festival

Creative Direction // Aron Filkey
Art Direction // Aron Filkey, Mate Moro
Photography // Mate Moro

This was a project for a fictional festival on literature and film. The festival was named after István Örkény, the founder of the Hungarian grotesque-prose, and was held on the anniversary of what would have been his 100th birthday in 2012. The visual nature of the image was inspired by his absurd novels.

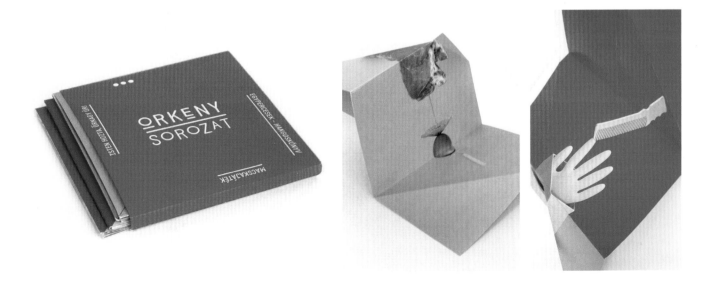

Grow

Styling // Aliki Kirmitsi
Retouching // The Forge UK
Photography // Ania Wawrzkowicz

Grow London was the first complete Gardening Fair held in London's Hampstead Heath in the summer of 2014; the fair brought together a vast variety of traders, gardeners and outdoor lovers. The aim for the image was to best reflect the various groups of people and the creativity and happiness gardening brings.

Wool

<u>Styling</u> // Aliki Kirmitsi
<u>Photography</u> // Ania Wawrzkowicz

Wool was a collaborative work between set designer Aliki Kirmitsi and photographer Ania Wawrzkowicz, reflecting the fragility and delicacy of space by using a clean canvas and some delicate threads to narrate more with less.

Apoteket

Ad Agency // Kollo
Photography // Carl Kleiner

Apoteket is a national pharmaceuticals retailing enterprise in Sweden. Photographer Carl Kleiner created two innovative characters to promote their new series of toothbrushes, toothpastes and mouthwashes.

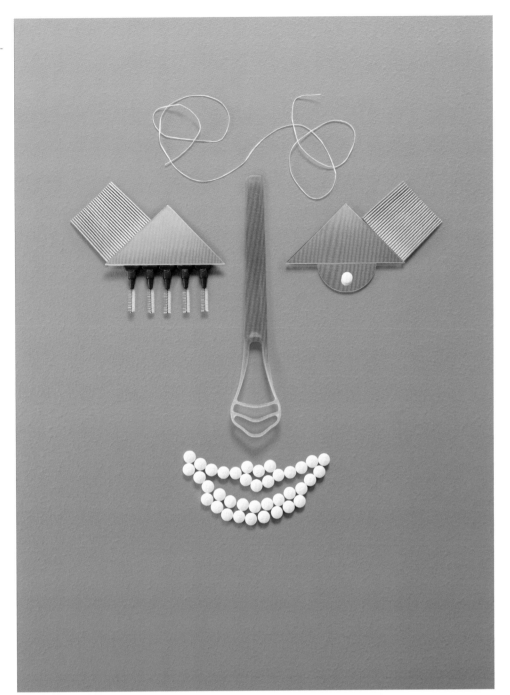

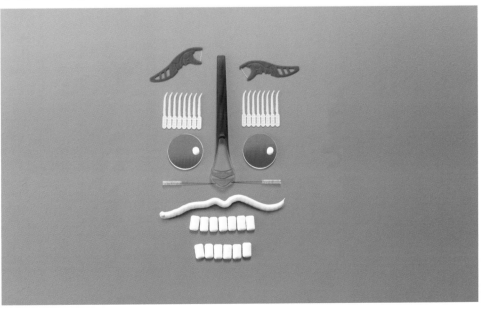

Fashion Houses

....

Set Design // Talib Choudhry
Photography // Victoria Ling

This editorial was commissioned by *Elle Decoration* to
show the interiors ranges from high end fashion houses.
Working with stylist Talib Choudhry, photographer Victoria
Ling worked on a flexible set to tie together the varied
objects. By creating a selection of flats, cubes and
spheres with a gentle colour palette the images were
bought together and depth was given to the images.

Play

Art Direction // Bianca Wendt
Set Design & Prop Styling //
Linnea Apelqvist
Photography // Victoria Ling

Victoria Ling shoots regularly for
Viewpoint, a trend predictions
magazine, and they have some great
themes and very creative shoots. This
commission was a collaboration with
Linnea Apelqvist and Bianca Wendt
for the 'Play' issue, using Joke Shop
toys as a reference.

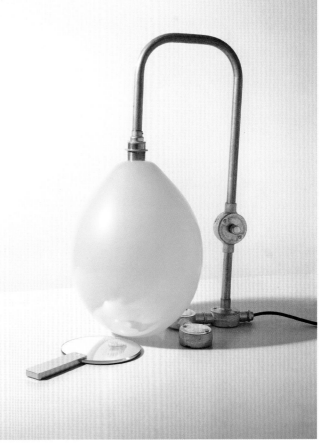

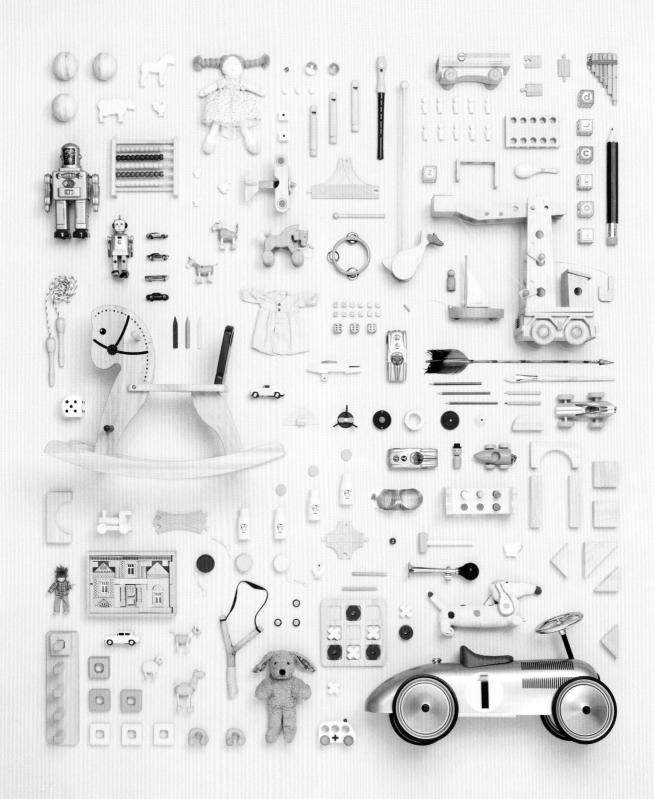

Order

Creative Direction // Winkreative
Art Direction // Darren Rogers @ Winkreative
Styling // Aliki Kirmitsi
Photography // Todd McLellan

A series of images created for the advertising campaign led by Winkreative agency for a bank consulting company in Switzerland. Using chaotic environments, such as a kitchen, a garden or a child room, set designer Aliki Kirmitsi and a group of creatives portrayed them in complete order form reflecting the ability of the company to preform in chaotic situations and produced absolute order and harmony.

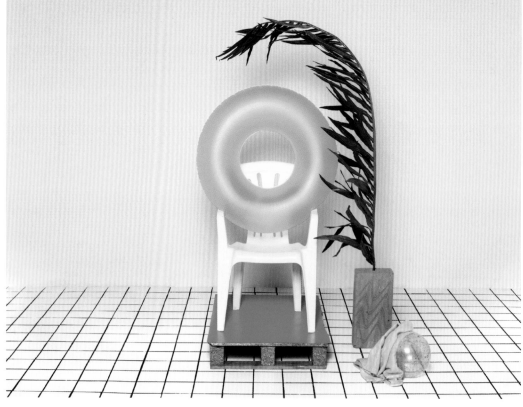

Pool Party

<u>Creative Direction</u> // Jess Bonham, Anna Lomax
<u>Art Direction</u> // Jess Bonham, Anna Lomax
<u>Set Design</u> // Anna Lomax
<u>Photography</u> // Jess Bonham

Part of a series of work around the idea of Pure Filth created for Pick Me Up Selects at Somerset House. Set designer Anna Lomax has amassed a serious collection of things that she treasures more than anything else. The works in this series were inspired by her collections.

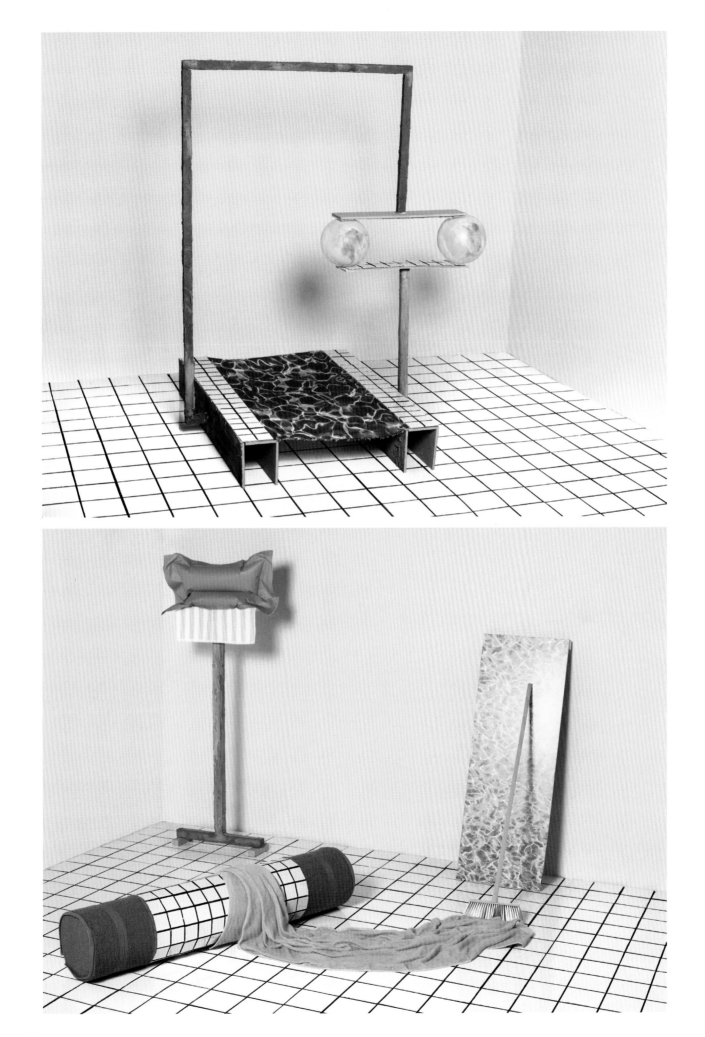

Surrealist Winner

<u>Styling</u> // Elena Mora
<u>Photography</u> // Patrick Viebranz

Set designer Elena Mora wanted to make some pictures using visual contrasts, something surreal, together with some real elements, like a feather, or a branch from a tree. Something vintage, together with a pop colour. Every scene described things which were happening without an order. It was like a field where you could develop your own story.

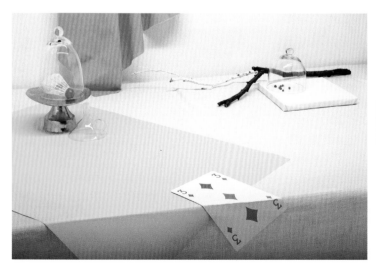

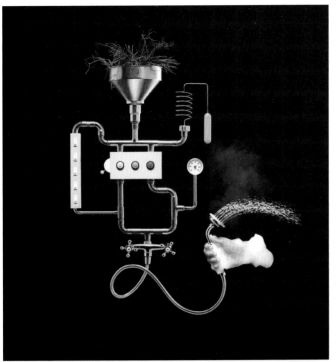

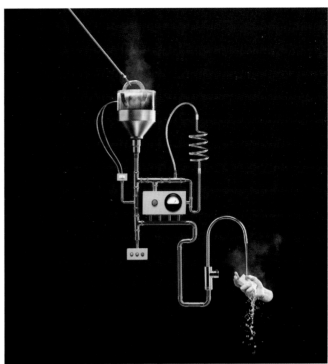

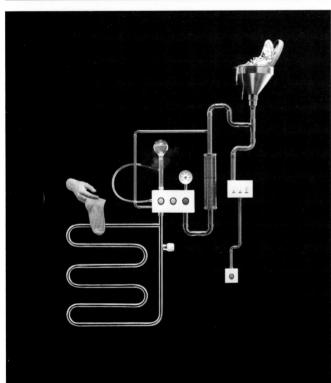

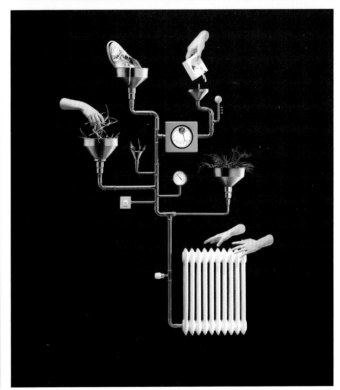

Fjärrvärme

Ad Agency // TBWA
Photography // Carl Kleiner

International advertising agency TBWA commissioned photographer Carl Kleiner to launch this project for the promotional campaign of Fjärrvärme.

Fit For Fun

<u>Styling</u> // Elena Mora
<u>Photography</u> // Karsten Wegener

Fit For Fun is a German magazine about sport and health. Set designer Elena Mora was asked to think about how to show some beauty products, thought to be used after sport. There were 3 different groups, which were one for teenagers, one for younger people and one for older people. She decided to paint and describe these sport elements which are mainly related to these 3 different groups.

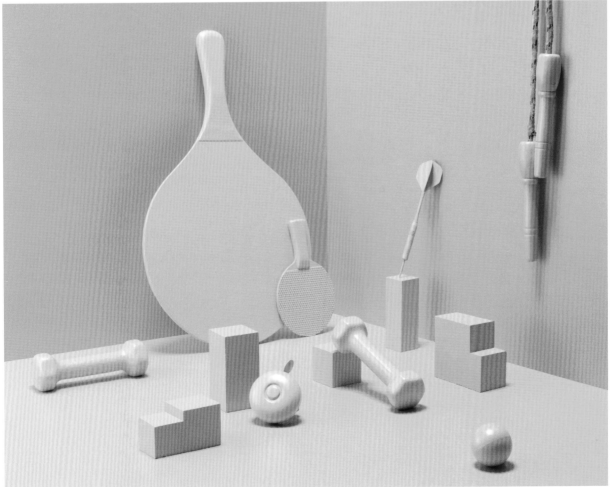

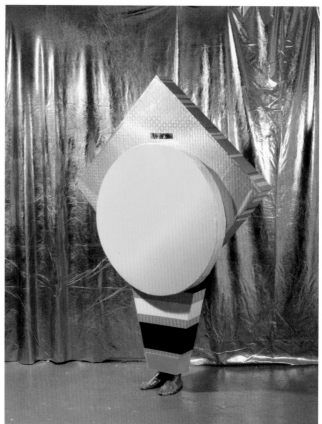

Religion

<u>Set Design</u> // Anna Lomax

In this project set designer Anna Lomax created something unique, artistic and religious by gathering together the old and the new, the absurd and the humorous, the bizarre and the unrecognizable.

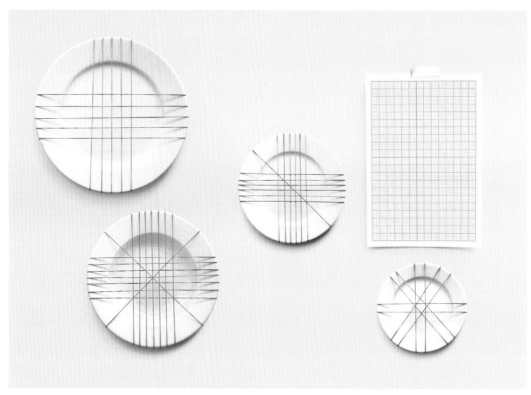

AVÔ

<u>Design Agency</u> // Studio AH-HA
<u>Creative Direction</u> // Catarina Carreiras, Carolina Cantante
<u>Art Direction</u> // Catarina Carreiras, Carolina Cantante
<u>Design</u> // Sam Baron, Charlotte Juillard, Giorgia Zanelatto,
         Diogo Alves, Jade Folawyio, Joao Valente,
         Ryu Yamamoto, Mariana Carreiras, Martinho Pita
<u>Styling</u> // Diogo Alves
<u>Model Maker</u> // Francisca Ramalho
<u>Photography</u> // Diogo Alves / Studio AH-HA

AVÔ is a collection of objects inspired by a grandfather's long and lost paper collection. Studio AH-HA challenged their friends and favourite designers to design an object inspired by one of the different pieces of paper kept in these exquisite piles of paper. Presented in an exhibition at Sam Baron & Co's gallery in Lisbon, the result was an eclectic collection and a humble homage, which showcased the work of a new generation of designers.

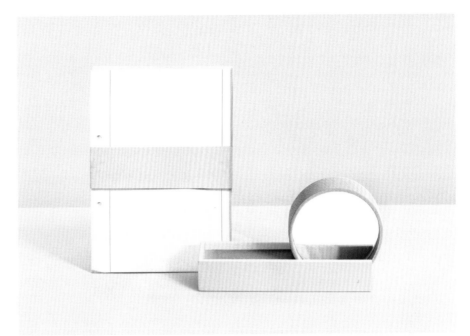

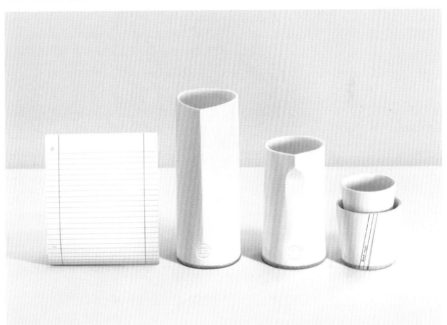

CONFIDENCIAL

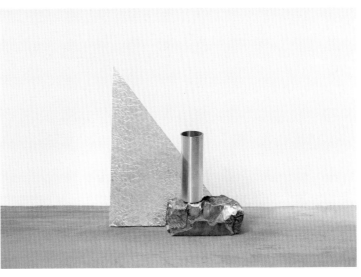

Mercado

....

<u>Creative Direction</u> // Sam Baron
<u>Art Direction</u> // Catarina Carreiras, Carolina Cantante
<u>Design</u> // Catarina Carreiras, Carolina Cantante
<u>Styling</u> // Diogo Alves
<u>Model Maker</u> // Diogo Alves
<u>Photography</u> // Diogo Alves / Studio AH-HA

Communication project, packaging and website for a Portuguese craft online shop.

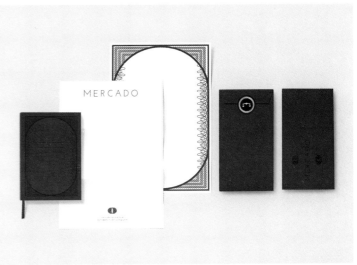

SOT Branding

Design Agency // RM&CO
Design // Pete Rossi
Photography // Dai Williams

Shapes of Things (SOT) is a new and revolutionary UK based surface and product design company for which RM&CO created a branding system based on pure geometric shapes inspired by the brand name itself. Developed to portray the "SOT" ethos and focus on a "back to basics" theme, RM&CO utilized geometric forms and structures with playful results. RM&CO also art directed the first launch campaign, "13," to bring the Shapes of Things brand to life and will develop a preceding campaign (e.g. "12," "11") every year.

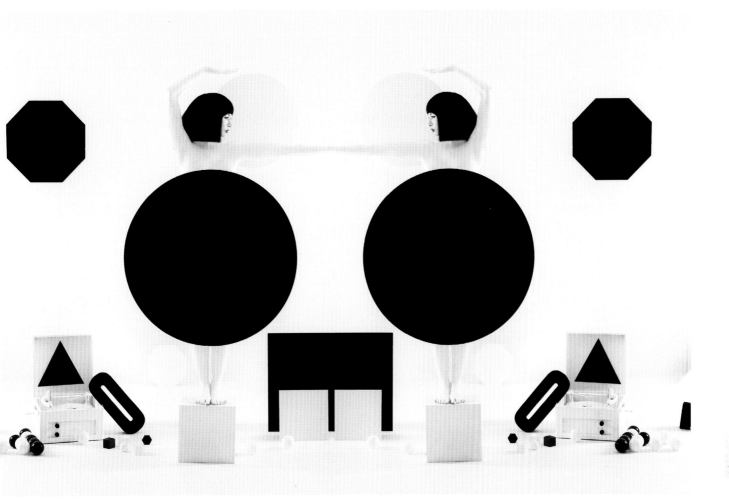

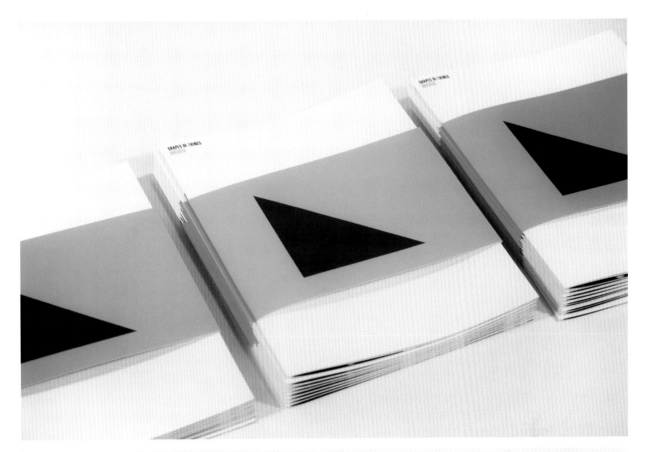

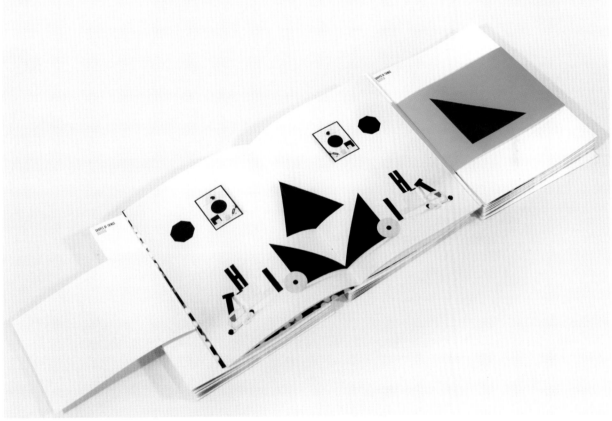

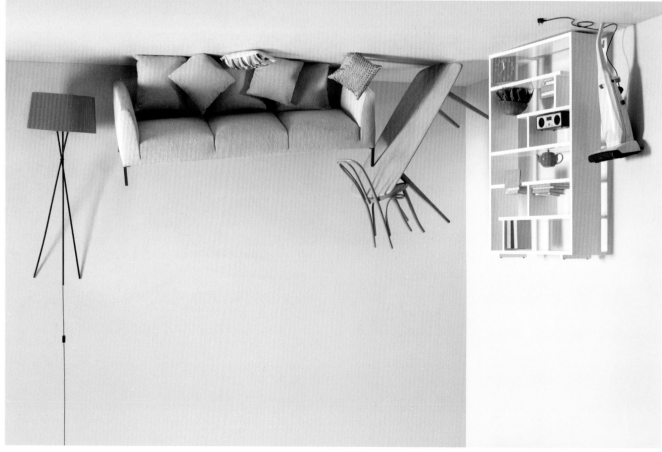

Avios

Ad Agency // 101London
Set Design // Evelina Kleiner
Photography // Carl Kleiner

Avios was commissioned for an Avios ad campaign, a company experienced in an air travel and leisure points reward system. Using the company's slogan "Anything Can Fly," photographer Carl Kleiner organised everyday items suspended in mid-flight against a sky blue background. The results were these visually tricky and gravity-defying compositions. Each thing seen in the photographs can be acquired through the Avios system by cashing in accumulated points.

Real Life at Work

....

<u>Design Agency</u> // W+K UK
<u>Art Direction</u> // Karen Jane
<u>Design</u> // Emily Forgot, Laurie D,
  Karen Jane

The Hello Neighbour team of Wieden+Kennedy UK collaborated with graphic artist Emily Forgot and Laurie D to create Real Life at Work, a new living, breathing workspace specially created for their window to give the outside world a look at the way they work.

Movers and Shakers

Styling // Elena Mora
Photography // Patrick Viebranz

These pictures were made as set for a fashion shooting. Set designer Elena Mora wanted to create dreamy and playful environments, letting the model play with it.

TECHNE: The Visual Workshop

Design Agency // PARTY Tokyo
Creative Direction // Masashi Kawamura
Art Direction // Yuni Yoshida

TECHNE: The Visual Workshop was a creative educational TV show for NHK ETV, Japan's biggest public broadcaster. Every episode introduces one visual technique (such as stop-motion), then challenges creators to produce a film using that technique. The viewers can get inspired and become interested in film-making not only through watching famous masterpieces, but also by witnessing renowned filmmakers' process of creating a film. All 3 episodes made it onto the Twitter trends.

221

Sarah May's Portfolio

<u>Design</u> // Sarah May

Sarah May is an art director and set designer. Trained as a fine artist, she draws inspiration from a wide range of influences which go on to inform her bright and conceptual approach. Establishing her studio in 2007, she has an extensive client list , including *British Vogue, Dazed* and *Confused, Japanese Vogue, Details,* Camper, Pepsi, Coca Cola, Paul Smith, Nike, French Connection and American Apparel.

i-D Bauhda

<u>Photography</u> // Namsa Leuba
<u>Clothes</u> // COMME des GARCONS

The *i-D Magazine* 'BAUHDA' editorial was inspired by the brand's own avant-garde and unconventional designs. "It's a series that came from African inspiration, from the Bauhaus and Dada shapes and geometrical structures. I like to associate fashion, culture, and the cloth itself to my projects," said the photographer Namsa Leuba.

Daydream
Nation Lookbook AW13

....

<u>Art Direction</u> // Jing, Timmy, Jason @ Little Thing
<u>Make-up</u> // Karen Yiu
<u>Hair</u> // Ritz Lam, Alex Chu @ The Look Studio
<u>Model</u> // Polina K @ Mission
<u>Photography</u> // Ken Ngan @ Flesh & Torso

Promotional campaign for Fashion Arts House
Daydream Nation's 2013 autumn/winter collection
'Neverending Story.'

Daydream Nation Lookbook SS12

....

<u>Creative Direction</u> // The Light Particles, Jing Wong
<u>Photography</u> // The Light Particles

Promotional campaign for Fashion Arts House Daydream Nation's 2012 spring/summer collection 'The Show Must Go On.'

INDEX

A

Adrian & Gidi

www.adrian-gidi.com

Adrian & Gidi represents the collaborative work of Adrian Woods & Gidi van Maarseveen, a young photography duo based in Amsterdam, the Netherlands. They first met at the Royal Academy of Arts in The Hague, where they both graduated in 2010. Since 2012 they have been working together with a playful and experimental approach towards work, specialising in tangible still life and product photography.

P046-047, P060-P061, P062, P096, P112-113, P118-119

Alexis Facca

www.alexisfacca.com

Alexis Facca comes from south of France but he's now based in Brussels, Belgium. Alexis is a paper and set designer who spends most of his time to misuse objects to build new stuff. He already worked with clients like Converse, Universal Music, Michelin, etc.

P050, P056-057, P124-125

Aliki Kirmitsi

www.alikikirmitsi.com

Aliki Kirmitsi was born in Cyprus; she studied Spatial Design in London where she now lives and works as a Set Designer for photography and installations. Her clients include: Sony, *The Week Fashion Magazine*, *The Sunday Times*, *The Guardian*, *Elle Deco Pl*, *Maison Figaro CY*, *Avant Garde Press*, Winkreative, John Lewis, Marks & Spencer, Alessi, Ink, IcoDesign, John Brown, Octopus Publications, Harris & Wilson Publishing, Vodaphone, etc. When designing a set, she believes in exploring the stories that objects and spaces hold and the tales of the interaction between them.

P126-127, P173, P186-187, P188, P194-195

Amy Harris

www.amy-harris.co.uk

From her East London studio, Amy creates a variety of illustrations, sets and bespoke objects from an assortment of materials. Inspired by geometry, folk art, minimalism, colour, pattern and much more in between, her designs have a playful approach to ideas and an attention to detail throughout.

Egyption pyramids, giant toy soldiers, colourful typography, busy little people, plant life and geometric creations all feature in the inventive worlds and subtle compositions that make up her designs. From window displays and handmade objects to events, websites and editorial projects, her work has caught the eye of clients including *The Guardian*, Supermarket Sarah, CHI & Partners, *Esquire Magazine*, Mr Porter and Tatty Devine.

P042, P043, P048-049

Anna Lomax

www.annalomax.com

Anna Lomax is a maker and collector. After graduating from Brighton University in Illustration in 2007, she didn't continue her career of illustration but involved herself into set design. Fascinated by the bizarre, pop-culture, folk art, pound shops and other peoples junk, she creates work with strong personality of novelty, uniqueness and weirdness. She works within the field of art direction and set design from small scale still life through to large scale installation using a range of mediums for varied clients including Nike, Becks, Topshop, Selfridges, Clarks Originals, Converse, Vauxhall Cars, *Vogue UK, Creative Review, Garage Magazine, Viewpoint Magazine, Elle Collections* and *The Independent*.

P070-071, P072-073, P082-083, P088-089, P099, P102-103, P120, P176-177, P196-197, P202-203

Aron Filkey

http://aronfilkey.com

Aron Filkey is a Hungarian graphic designer specialising in hand-made and analogue solutions of graphic works. His artistic philosophy is to find and expose the relationship between the machine and the human being. He obtained his bachelor diploma from the graphic design department of the Moholy-Nagy University of Art and Design, Budapest Hungary with his thesis addressing the post-digital culture. Upon completion of his bachelor degree, Aron entered the master's program at the graphic design department of the Moholy-Nagy University of Art and Design. After the first semester, he received a scholarship to the University der Kunste Berlin in Berlin, Germany and spent half a year at the visual communication department during the spring and summer of 2013. With over seven years of experience in the field, he has collaborated with a number of artists in the file including photographers, directors, and visual artists.

P030-031, P064-065, P104-105, P106-107, P184-185

B

Ben Pogue

www.benpogue.com

Ben Pogue is a visual artist who works primarily within the discipline of still-life photography. Ben is known for his fresh, minimal approach to photography. His restraint in composition, sophisticated use of colour and ability to retain the tactile qualities of his subjects has allowed him to collaborate with the foremost creative publications and brands. He has contributed to various publications, such as *T Magazine, The New York Times Style Magazine, US Vogue, Teen Vogue, Details, Esquire* and *V Magazine*. His advertising clients include; Chanel, MAC Cosmetics, Jil Sander, Nike, Reebok, H&M, and Uniqlo.

P180-181

Bond

www.bond.fi

Bond is a versatile creative agency founded by designers with different specialties. Their skill set covers strategic, graphic, product, digital and retail design. Their creative work always starts at the core of a brand, based on which they create a lot of practical ideas for brand behavior. Together with the client, they identify the best ones.

P174-175

C

Carl Kleiner

www.carlkleiner.com

Carl Kleiner is a Swedish image maker. He photographs still life, portraits, fashion and life style, and directs moving image work. Carl embraces colours, geometry and graphical composition in the images he creates. His clients include Ikea, Häagen-Dazs, Uniqlo, Sony, *Wallpaper** and *The New York Times Magazine*. Carl lives in Stockholm with his wife and son.

P038-039, P063, P084-085, P098, P182-183, P189, P199, P214-215

Carolin Wanitzek

www.carolinwanitzek.de

Carolin Wanitzek is a communication designer based in Mannheim, Germany. She was studying communication design at the Mannheim University of Applied Sciences and is mainly working in the field of photography, corporate design and editorial design. She has a passion for handmade graphics and creating three-dimensional illustrations made out of paper or other objects.

P032-033, P040, P132-133, P134-135, P144-145, P154-155, P158-159

Christian Ashton

www.christianashton.co.uk

Christian Ashton is a graphic designer based in London. His main focus is creating graphical props, dressing, branding and design for film, television, magazine, corporate and all other things graphical. He has worked with many different companies such as Marvel, Disney, Universal Studios, Vogue, Time Out, in many different aspects of graphic design.

P036-037

Cris Wiegandt

www.criswiegandt.com

Cris Wiegandt is a Brazilian artist of German descent. Growing up in the ultimate Brazilian metropolis Sao Paulo, it's no wonder that she couldn't help but travel the world and by now be settled in another huge and creative city: Berlin. Since 2011 she is a freelance director, animator and designer and has worked for different clients like Disney, Kindernet Nickelodeon, *Nylon Magazine* and Commerzbank. Her work is a mixture of paper craft illustration, stop motion, 2D animation and music videos. It is a delicate work, meticulous and charming.

P034-035, P044, P128-129

D

Daydream Nation

www.daydream-nation.com

Daydream Nation is a Fashion Arts House founded in 2006. Aside from being an international fashion label, Daydream Nation is celebrated for its cross-disciplinary collaborations with other art forms including theatre, dance, music, film and visual arts. Alongside its own collection of clothing and accessories, it features the work of local artists and indie bands, and runs a program of creative workshops, events and happenings.

P230-231, P232

E

Elena Mora

www.elenamora.com

Elena Mora is an Italian freelance stylist and set designer currently living in Hamburg. Elena studied at Politecninco di Milano; afterwards, she moved to Finland, where she experienced cold days and long summer nights while studying at the Lapland University. She then moved to Berlin and worked at Blotto Design and Jutojo. She has also been working at the Milan-based publishing house Mousse Publishing. In the last years she had the chance to work for clients such as *Wallpapaer**, *Der Spiegel, Esquire Holland*, Volkswagen, Audi and many others.

P051, P068-069, P092-093, P114-115, P198, P200-201, P218-219

F

FABRICA

www.fabrica.it

FABRICA is a communication research centre. Located in Treviso, it is an integral part of the Benetton Group. FABRICA was established in 1994, and offers a one-year study scholarship, complete with accommodation and travel expenses to and from Italy, to an extremely diverse community of researchers from across the globe. Their range of fields is equally varied, and includes design, communication, photography, interaction, video, music, journalism and media. FABRICA is based in a 17th-century villa that has been restored and enlarged by Japanese architect Tadao Ando.

P100-101

G

Greg Barth

www.gregbarth.tv

Designer turned director Greg Barth is an award winning artist and director from Geneva, Switzerland, currently based in London. Greg specialises in design driven projects ranging from video art and Installations to Music Videos and TV advertisements. His passion for strong, often surreal concepts, and contemporary minimal aesthetics have brought him to work for renowned international clients, get published in prestigious design books, and be strongly featured in the visual industry's leading blogs and websites.

P166-167, P178-179

Grégoire Alexandre

www.gregoirealexandre.com

Normandy-born Grégoire Alexandre now stationed in Paris. Cinema was his first interest, but he became more comfortable with photography since it gave him a greater sense of control and allowed him to take something out of reality without having to set it up first.

P045, P074, P075

H

Hernan Paganini

www.hernanpaganini.com.ar

Hernan Paganini is an ambitious Argentinean designer, painter, sculptor, and teacher. In his artwork, each new piece of colour or matter is not a symbol on its own, but rather a fragment through which he shares a part of his own being. He poetically shares his inspiration as "The length, width and depth of life, with all its various and endless possibilities." Hernan said, "I believe that creativity is the synchronicity of the universe – the translucent and opaque multiple connections between all beings and stars that inhabit the infinite galaxy of those vertices. Everything you need is here in this every day."

P076-079, P080-081

J

Jess Bonham

www.jessbonham.co.uk

Jess Bonham is a still-life photographer, working primarily in the area of editorial and commercial product photography. Graduating in 2007 from The University of Brighton with a degree in illustration Jess went on to work as a prop maker before working in the photography industry as a lighting assistant. She now focuses on creating images based around a love for pattern and precision, reinvention, curious correlations and seeking order out of chaos. Her work touches upon the world of sculpture and installation, with an injection of humour and surprise. Previous clients include Kenzo, Selfridges, Ford, Jaguar, Belvedere, Chambord, *UK Vogue*, Miss Vogue, Twin, Aston Martin, *German Wired*, *Wonderland*, *Garage* and *The Gourmand*.

P082-083, P088-089, P099, P102-103, P108-109, P120, P142-143, P172, P176-177, P196-197

Jonas Sellami

www.sellagraphic.com

Based in Nantes (France), Jonas Sellami (a.k.a. "Sella") is a young designer who officiates in multiple areas and enjoys playing with shapes. In parallel to it, Jonas maintains a close relationship with music and tries to melt as much as possible these fields.

P162-163, P170-171

K

Kyle Bean

www.kylebean.co.uk

Kyle Bean is an artist, designer and illustrator with a passion for craft and conceptual thinking. He creates playful, imaginative work for a variety of clients that appear in editorial and commercial projects as well as installations for luxury fashion brands and events. Kyle's work is usually characterised by a whimsical and meticulous reappropriation of everyday materials and handcrafted techniques.

P140

L

Leta Sobierajski

http://letasobierajski.net

Leta Sobierajski is a multidisciplinary designer and art director living and working in New York City. She combines mediums in design, photography, art, and styling to develop tangible compositions for print, digital, and motion. She has been recognized as a top 20 under 30 designer in *Print Magazine*'s New Visual Artists issue in 2014. She has collaborated with IBM, Google, Partners & Spade, The Art Director's Club, Ogilvy & Mather, *NYLON Magazine*, Lynda.com, and many others.

P110-111, P136-137, P160-161, P168-169

Linnea Apelqvist

www.linneaapelqvist.com

Born in Sweden, Linnea Apelqvist now lives and works in London, where she also grew up. She studied Set Design for Stage and Screen at Wimbledon College of Art. Clients include Ted Baker, *Cyclist Magazine, Wonderland Magazine, Tatler Russia*, Modalu, *Viewpoint Magazine, The New Review/Independent*, Mono-Zine, *British Vogue, 1883 Magazine*, Argos, *TANK Magazine*, Swarovski, John Lewis,

Marie Claire, GAP, Aurbach & Steele, Monki, Kikimora, Ink Publishing, Nikos Nicolaou, Gravitonas, *Plaza Magazine*, WAD, Wolf & Badger, among others.

P066-067, P094-095, P097, P192-193

Luke J Albért

www.lukejalbert.co.uk

The whimsical world of still life photographer Luke J Albért is saturated with colour, happiness and playful product that seems to leap from the page with glee. His mixed media collages burst with abstract cut-outs, while his prop styling transforms spatulas and wooden spoons into dancing figurines.

Luke has mastered the challenge of the still life photographer, presenting the object as accessible and easily understood, while engaging the audience in a captivating and surrealist story. His use of vibrant colour in complementary abstract backgrounds is similar to the works of abstract synchromism painters, who proclaimed colour as the basis of expression and experience. He has created stunning visuals for Monki, Philips, Monoprix, Galleries Lafayete, *Observer Magazine*, and others.

P090-091, P156-157

M

mililitros

www.mililitros.com

M. Laura Benavente (a.k.a. "mililitros") is a Fine Arts graduate who specialises in photography, but essentially her work is about providing creative solutions to visual ideas, from photography right through to publishing projects. As each project presents its own unique challenges she ensures that each is tackled with innovative solutions by combining the different disciplines she works with, which is what makes her work so diverse and multifaceted. She produces photographic reproductions of other artists' artwork and exhibitions as well as fashion and

commercial photography. She also does illustrations, photo set designs, paper crafts, art direction and anything related to the world of photography and creative work.

P122-123, P138-139

Marisa Fjärem

www.marisafjarem.com

Marisa Fjärem works as a prop and set designer for advertising, film and window display and makes scenic interiors and spatial experiences for events and stages. She has a background as the Creative Director, illustrator and concept founder of clothing brand Monki where her story of the Monkis and their world made her interested in storytelling design. After Monki, Marisa started to work more three dimensional while working with the JoAnn Tan Studio designing and producing the window display for Swedish department store NK. Since fall 2012 she has been freelancing for clients such as H&M, Sony, Weekday, Triwa, IKEA, Bocuse d'Or, Oriflame, Breuninger, Wilfa among others. She also creates the stage design for some of famous Sweden artists such as The Knife and Veronica Maggio. She likes her work to communicate a story, make magical imaginary worlds and build concepts that make the viewer inspired, confused and happy.

P086-087

N

Namsa Leuba

http://namsaleuba.com

Namsa Leuba was born in 1982 from a Guinean mother and a Swiss father. During the past 3 years, her research focused on African identity through Western eyes. Her work has been published in numerous magazines, including *I-D, Numéro, KALEIDOSCOPE, Foam, Interview, Vice Magazine, New York Magazine, Wallpaper**,

Libération, British Journal of Photography, European Photography, etc. Namsa has also received notable international recognitions.

P228-229

O

Oksana Valentelis

www.oksanavalentelis.com

An art director and a fine artist, Oksana Valentelis was raised in the post Soviet climes of Eastern Europe, where she got her first taste for art in the regimented and strict environment of Soviet Art School. From the age of 16 she studied Philosophy in London and later Graphic Design at Central St Martins. Oksana sells her prints via Nelly Duff gallery in London's East End.

P058-059

Oliver Stenberg

http://oliverstenberg.tumblr.com

Oliver Stenberg is a Montreal/Toronto-based set designer, represented by L'ELOI. He is known for his strict attention to detail with a very clean and modern aesthetic. Oliver more commonly finds his inspiration from nature and architecture than from ever changing trends. L'ELOI is a Montreal-based agency that represents true artists in the fields of photography. Film, styling, set design, and hair and makeup.

P116-117

P

PARTY

www.prty.jp

Creative Lab PARTY focuses on experimenting with design that utilizes technology, catering to the 'networked' world and the 'maker' culture. With offices in Tokyo and New York, PARTY engages in various design projects from around the globe, ranging from brand communication, product, service, content to event, and space design. Aside from the commissioned work, they also invest their energies into research and development, building their product prototypes that cross over the boundaries of design and art.

By liberating themselves from the usual creative process, and through discovering talents from unexplored fields, they constantly aim to create work that the world has never seen before. PARTY believes in the possibilities of design and technology.

P220-223

PRIM PRIM

www.primprim.lt

PRIM PRIM is a visual communication design studio with a strong imaginative goal to create authentic designs where concept, visuality and aesthetics match all together. The key aspect of their style is a minimalistic attitude toward graphics – a clean, light, aesthetic and logical design. Visual media creates a lot of noise in our environment, so they strive to bring cleanness and order to life.

Their creative path is also heavily influenced by their country Lithuania, and some of their home country of Lithuania, and some of their projects are based on ethnic Lithuanian-Baltic culture. They enjoy experimenting with combinations of fresh and "up to date" design combined with more archaic content and forms, but even then they remain faithful to their aesthetic ideals.

P018-025

R

RM&CO

www.rossimazzei.com

RM&CO, founded in 2013 by Pete Rossi (ADC YG 9) and Alfio Mazzei, is an independent, multi-disciplinary graphic design, visual communication and branding consultancy with studios based in Glasgow, London and Balerna, Switzerland. RM&CO believes in ideas and socially engaging work coupled with a simple philosophy based on intelligent, crafted and original design that makes a difference and solves problems effectively. Their work is informed by the process and development inherent within any one given project – driven by ideas and not relying on aesthetics and style. They are firm believers in pushing boundaries, but their meticulous approach, based on research, process and development allows them to serve their client's purpose with passion, detail, dedication and love to find the right and relevant solutions to a wide variety of projects and commissions. RM&CO joined the Design Business Association (DBA) in 2014 and has been awarded and recognised by ADC, D&AD, Graphis and Red Dot.

P210-213

Roberto Ruiz

http://robertoruiz.eu

Born in Zaragoza on 26th January 1976, Roberto Ruiz lives in Barcelona. He had a bachelor degree in Fine Arts from the University of Cuenca and a master degree "Art, Territory and Media Culture" from the University of Barcelona. His work has been published in numerous magazines, including *Neo2 Magazine*, *Tendencias Magazine*, *B-guided*, *ICON de El País*, *Rojo Magazine*, *Wee Magazine*, etc. His work has been selected in Crea Arte Emergente (Sala Coma Estadella, Lleida), Bac (CCCB, Barcelona), Muestra de arte joven (Instituto aragonés de la juventud, Zaragoza), La ilusión del pirata (Sant Andreu Contemporani, Barcelona), Situación Lérida (La Panera, Lleida) and exhibited in Vierter Stock (Berlín), galería Franco de Toledo (Barcelona), galería Espace Ample (Barcelona), galería Loft (Barcelona), galería fotográfica Fotodeluxe (Lérida). His client list includes La Mallorquina, La Comercial, Florida 135, Cherry Heel, The Rice-co and many others.

P146-147, P148-149, P150-151, P152-153

Ryan Romanes

www.ryanromanes.co.nz

Ryan Romanes is a New Zealand born designer living in Melbourne, Australia. Focusing on branding and art direction, he collaborates with design studios and freelances directly with clients. Ryan has worked in Auckland, Dubai and interned with Sagmeister & Walsh in New York City before relocating to Melbourne. He now works with local and international clients of all business backgrounds for graphic design and image making projects.

P054-055

S

Sarah May

www.sarahmaystudio.com/

Sarah May is an art director and set designer. Trained as a fine artist, she draws inspiration from a wide range of influences which go on to inform her bright and conceptual approach. Establishing her studio in 2007, she has an extensive client list, including _British Vogue, Dazed and Confused, Japanese Vogue, Details,_ Camper, Pepsi, Coca Cola, Paul Smith, Nike, French Connection and American Apparel.

P224-227

SNASK

www.snask.com

SNASK believes in standing out and has opinions to stand up for. To be a part of the present time and have the gaze nailed to tomorrow. SNASK believes in telling stories and really dares to be personal. They constantly question and challenge social conventions. They are not afraid of making enemies, because they believe that a brand, with obvious enemies, becomes clear and distinguishable, and will have millions of fans and followers.

P009-013, P014-017, P026-029

Studio AH-HA

www.studioahha.com

Studio AH-HA is a communication and graphic design studio established in 2011 by Carolina Cantante and Catarina Carreiras. The studio pursues varied creative interests across a variety of mediums: from brand strategy to interior design, naming and identity work, advertising, new media, traditional and fine print, retail and product design, photography and illustration.

P204-207, P208-209

V

Victoria Ling

www.victorialing.com

Victoria Ling is based in London and predominantly shoots still life. Her aesthetic is clean and minimalist, with keen attention to detail, texture and colour. She came to photography from a fine art degree and an interest in pinhole cameras. She has been shooting since 2008, recent clients including Burberry, Diageo, John Lewis, _Viewpoint, Wired, Wallpaper*,_ Tatler, Marie Claire, Casio, and FranklinTill.

P041, P052-P053, P121, P190-191, P192-193

W

Wieden+Kennedy London

http://wklondon.com

Wieden+Kennedy London is part of the world's only creatively-led, independent global agency network. Founded in 1982, the agency has always focused on creating strong, provocative relationships between good companies and their customers. W+K was named Adweek's Global Agency Of The Year, Cannes Agency Of The Year 2012, and Creativity and Cannes Independent Agency Of The Year in 2013.

P216-217

Wendy van Santen

www.wendyvansanten.com

Wendy van Santen is an Amsterdam-based photographer. Her biggest passion is still photography. Her images can be recognised by their minimalist composition, use of colour and conceptual message. She's a perfectionist that loves to carefully construct her still series in the studio. When working on her images she loses all sense of time and place. Her goal is to create images that surprise people and inspire them to look at the world in a different way. She works for magazines, newspapers and advertising agencies.

P130-131, P141, P164-165

ACKNOWLEDGEMENTS

We would like to express our gratitude to all of the designers and companies for their generous contribution of images, ideas, and concepts. We are also very grateful to many other people whose names do not appear in the credits but who made specific contributions and provided support. Without them, the successful completion of this book would not be possible. Special thanks to all of the contributors for sharing their innovation and creativity with all of our readers around the world. Our editorial team includes editor Zhaohong Yang and book designer Dongyan Wu, to whom we are truly grateful.